New Persp[ectives on] Classroo[m] Drama

New Perspectives on Classroom Drama

Gavin Bolton

SIMON & SCHUSTER
EDUCATION

First published in Great Britain in 1992 by
Simon & Schuster Education
Campus 400, Maylands Avenue
Hemel Hempstead, Herts HP2 7EZ

Typeset in 10pt Baskerville by Graphicraft Typesetters, Hong Kong
Printed in Great Britain by T.J. Press (Padstow) Ltd.

A catalogue reference for this book is available from the British Library

ISBN 0 7501 0195 4

This book is dedicated to Helen and Claire Bolton, my granddaughters, who are in the first stage of their education

Contents

Acknowledgements

The author and publisher would like to thank the following for permission to reproduce copyright materials:

H.M.S.O., for extracts from *The Teaching and Learning of Drama*; Oliver & Boyd (for the National Curriculum Council) for extracts from *The Arts 5–16*; Blackwell Education for extracts from *The GCSE Drama Coursebook* by Andy Kempe; Puffin for an extract from *The Silver Sword* by Ian Serraillier; and Penguin for the poem *Croft* by Stevie Smith from *The Collected Poems of Stevie Smith*.

Preface

One of the reasons I have enjoyed writing this book is that I have not felt bound by the rules of the 'academic game': I have not felt it necessary to demonstrate that I have read all the 'right' literature; I have only referred to other people's writings where they impinge directly on what I want to say.

Most of what I have to say does not spring from books at all, but from my own workshop and classroom practice. It is not, however, a book *about* that practice; my intention is to offer a theoretical framework. References to what I have done in the classroom are there as sources from which my theoretical thinking derives. The reader should be wary of seeing my description of lessons as models of recommended practice. What I am *trying* to advocate is a way of looking at classroom drama.

Classroom-based writing is going to become something of a rarity. Too many key appointments in teacher education institutions are currently being filled by people who have little real classroom experience, yet they are the ones who have time and, indeed, are required by their position to write. In some universities in North America the myth that evidence of doctoral research has greater validity than evidence of sound practice is being perpetuated, so that instead of a PhD being a proper culmination of years of teaching experience, it is not surprisingly seen by ambitious young people as the necessary *starting point* of their career. Great teachers like Dorothy Heathcote would not, of course, even get onto a short-list!

Gavin Bolton March 1991

1 A Basis for Drama

Aristotle characterised drama as **mimesis**. His interpreters have disagreed about his meaning: some have taken the term to mean **imitation** – what goes on on stage imitates what goes on in the world; others have taken it to mean **representation**, or even a **metaphor** for what goes on in the world. This latter I find more palatable than 'imitation'. Nevertheless, I believe it is the notion of drama as imitation that has had most influence on how we have trained our children in drama. Many teachers adopt this as their principal criterion: 'How close to a resemblance of "the world out there" is this child getting in his acting?'. I suggest in this chapter that imitation is a necessary but insufficient component of dramatic behaviour, that imitation alone is too restricting.

One can see how Aristotle, or anyone else, can arrive at the imitation theory. Drama is the one art form that looks like what goes on in real life, and the actors on stage are intent on making us laugh or cry about it. No doubt Aristotle, given a chance, would have argued about film in the same way. A continuum from concrete to abstract shows how the Arts can be placed in relation to each other, with drama at one extreme, through dance, sculpture, visual arts and poetry, to music as the most abstract at the other end. There is a sense in which all the Arts, even music, have a degree of dependence on imitation of the world as we know it – the relationship between sound and silence in the world around him/her is something felt and transformed by the musician. For the dramatist and actor the dependence is even more apparent. I shall start by looking at the various ways in which drama *is* dependent on the 'world out there'.

Drama as a social context

Let me begin with what happens in 'real life'. We give a label to most social situations. We say we have been to 'a meeting', 'a lecture' or 'a party', witnessed 'an accident', or had 'a heart-to-heart talk'. We may use these labels with confidence, secure in our assumption that most people involved would, if required, use the same labels. It is by such labelling that we have a feeling of control over our lives. No doubt we could go through a whole day identifying how we moved from one kind of social event to another. What we may not realise is that some or all of the participants in the listed social contexts 'worked at' establishing those various contexts; they probably also 'worked at' signalling to each other their tacit agreement that the event had run its course. (Or there may even be some tacit *dis*agreement about when a context should be terminated. As a lecturer I am not unfamiliar with the snapping shut of a notebook from a member of the student audience to signal 'It's coffee time'!) What is it that the participants are likely to be working at? It is the *mutually agreed but unspoken rules* that give meaning to the event.

Sometimes these rules are so familiar to us that we never give them a thought as we 'submit to' them. (Indeed, 'working at' is a phrase that suggests a degree of consciousness and effort that does not often apply. However, the sociologists' term for it, 'managing', is hardly any better. Perhaps 'making', 'setting' or 'creating' might be considered. Until something better crops up I will continue to use the phrase 'working at'). When we go to a meeting we adopt our 'attending a meeting' behaviour without any conscious effort. On the other hand, if we were to take on the role of chairperson for the first time, the rules of proper procedure would probably be uppermost in our minds. We would hope to make the role credible to the other people present, and to ourselves. In other words we would be **'building belief'**, a term not unfamiliar to many classroom drama practitioners. Even where the occasion is not as formal as a meeting, there are still implicit rules to help us *believe* in the nature of the social context. Four football-supporter friends out for a good time are likely to feel compelled to demonstrate that they are enjoying themselves, by making the 'right' kind of jokes, using the 'right' language, drinking the 'right' alcohol, making the 'right' level of noise, having the 'right' kind of swagger, etc. The rules are no less in evidence when one observes two academics engaged in colloquy over coffee in the corner of the senior common room. Even when you are *caught* by an event not of your own making, for example suddenly meeting someone you have not seen for ten years, there is a tacit code to do with assumptions about the previous relationship which both of you hurriedly adjust to. Woe betide you if in your bones you feel it is someone you should be greeting warmly, but you cannot quite place him/her. You experience that momentory insecurity of not knowing whether you are sounding over effusive or rather cold. You have not found the appropriate label – is it a past neighbour?, a colleague?, someone who used to serve in the local store?, a fellow drinker? or the spouse's cousin? If s/he can't remember who you are either, you will both be fishing around for some kind of warm but neutral exchange that you both hope will adequately meet those unspoken rules. *And* you'll both, no doubt, be searching for suitable 'exit' lines! You will 'imitate' whatever the closure conventions allow, just as you were dependent, initially, on 'copying' the salutational 'How are you?', with which we tend to open meetings of this kind.

In the above example the rules were negotiable, but even the most clearly-defined social context can have its rules upset so that its participants find it difficult to 'believe' in it. Someone fainting in church upsets the 'church' context, probably in direct proportion to the distance one is from the sufferer. Something similar happened to me last year in Victoria, British Columbia, when I was giving a lecture to a group of Social Studies teachers. A member of my class suddenly suffered his windpipe closing; he struggled for breath and went purple. Some members of the class who had been sitting taking notes took over the situation by thumping him on the back or going out to send for an ambulance; others, like me, backed away feeling that we had no role there. A few walked him downstairs to meet the ambulance. As the door closed on the rest of us there was a hiatus in the room, during which we were not sure which social context we were in. After a moment I signalled the restarting of our former lecture context and began to pick up the threads of what I had been talking about. Just at that moment the door burst open. In rushed four ambulance men saying, 'Where is he?'. They had entered the building by a back door, missing the patient at the front. So once again our 'safe' social context was disturbed and the rules of the 'lecture context' were broken.

I am trying to emphasise that, although we may not be aware that we have to 'work at' social situations, they are indeed fragile, but it is normally only when something goes wrong that we become aware of the effort we have been making. I am sure that when the Social Studies teachers and I returned (yet again!) to the *status quo ante*, we all put extra effort into displaying the trappings of such a context. By asking and answering questions, writing new notes, summarising what had gone before, etc. we felt reassured that we knew where we were once more! But, of course, this kind of social context is fairly easy to resume because the rules are so well defined – there is a hierarchical and procedural pattern that makes 'building belief' relatively easy. This is not the case in an informal event. Imagine what it is like when something goes wrong at a party – one guest is not on speaking terms with another guest, someone gets embarrassingly drunk or someone has bad news! Parties are fragile affairs at the best of times (all the participants have to play by the rules for it to have credibility), but trying to retrieve the party spirit after a disruption, when there is a long-faced guest, or when a surprising number say they must leave early requires considerable effort if people are really going to believe in it as a party.

The disruption of a social event does not have to be so 'dramatic'. If people are simply 'not in the mood' for a party, a 'heart-to-heart' talk or 'going dancing', or even if it is just *one* of the participants who is 'not in the mood', then establishing the context becomes more difficult. Participants must *submit themselves* to the social event for it to be truly believable. I am using the word 'submit' advisedly as suggesting something rather more than 'conform', but it should not be interpreted as just *passive* – one can be *active* once one has submitted. What is required is 'giving oneself' over to what is happening, whether it is making love, playing football, celebrating an anniversary or having a day out. If you are distracted by something else, even if you are busy *pretending* that what you are supposed to be doing has your full attention, it will not ring true for you, and probably not for anyone else involved. Only when you 'give yourself' to an event can you be said to be experiencing it. You 'let it happen' to you so that you can then continue to 'make it happen'. It is an act both active and passive – like a swimmer, both submitting to and yet in control of the water. You live spontaneously in the 'here and now' of the social event. There is an **existential** quality to the experiencing, where you are engaging with a social event from *inside* it. *This concept is also critical to an understanding of classroom drama.* I shall attempt to demonstrate in subsequent chapters how this existential quality, while occurring to a degree in Theatre Performance between actor and actor, and actor and audience, is a *necessary* feature of much classroom drama, specifically in that aspect of classroom work I shall refer to as 'dramatic playing' activity (Chapter 2, p. 11).

Let me finish this section on 'real-life' social contexts by noting that there tends to be a *time* dimension to most social events. Initially, an effort is often made among the participants to signal or 'describe' to each other what kind of event it is. We may 'work at' putting on our 'party behaviour' or at establishing that it is to be a formal meeting. As we relax into the event, however, the need to 'imitate' the conventionalised signals of how one is required to behave at a party or at a meeting evaporates. Then we are free to 'submit' to the existential experience, *unless*, as in my earlier anecdote (p. 3), something goes wrong. If this happens we have to resume the descriptive signalling behaviour, in order to redefine the social context. Pictorially, the sequence might look as follows. I have used a mixture of black and white shading for the figures. Black suggests the intention to *describe* or *signal* to other participants what the social context is. White suggests the intention to *submit* to the experience, once the kind of social context is established. Notice that the figures are never entirely one or the other. I am trying to convey a fluid state, subject to change as the social event becomes threatened or stabilised.

A 'real-life' social context

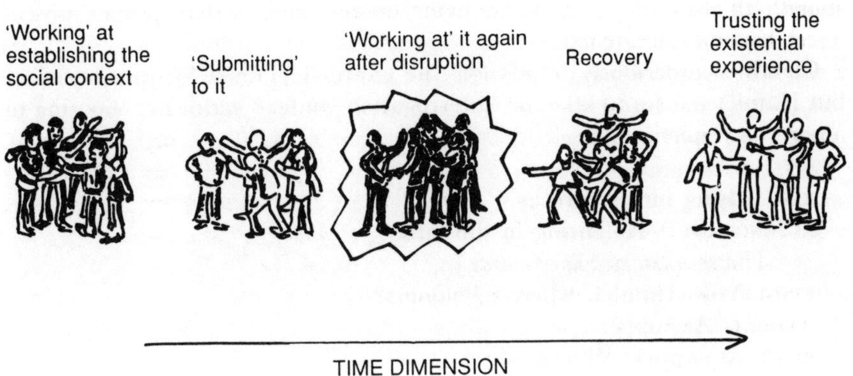

Diagrammatically, it would look like this:

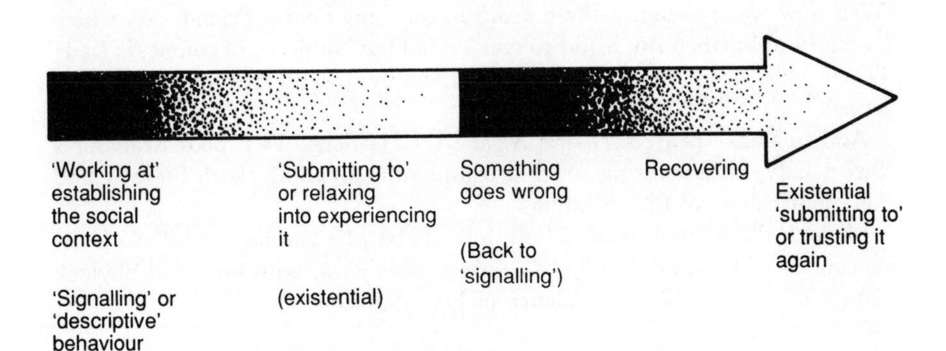

Dramatists imitate the making and breaking of social events

Playwrights, for the most part, model their scenes on clearly defined social contexts, so that the audience can pick up what is happening and characters can become established. Once the kind of social context is communicated to an audience, then from time to time a playwright may enjoy introducing devices that fracture that context. S/he typically uses a misunderstanding, someone not belonging, a character's deliberate attempt to misconstrue what the event is supposed to be, someone's mind being on something else, rules of etiquette being broken, etc., so that 'proper' procedures become threatened.

Claudius imperiously 'sends for' the guarded Hamlet for interrogation, but Hamlet refuses to take the 'interrogation context' seriously, choosing to ignore its implicit rules:

KING: Bring him before us.
ROSENCRANTZ: Ho! Bring in the lord.
[*Enter* HAMLET *with Guards.*]
KING: Now, Hamlet, where's Polonius?
HAMLET: At supper.
KING: At supper? Where?
HAMLET: Not where he eats, but where he is eaten. A certain convocation of politic worms are e'en at him.

Shakespeare, *Hamlet* Act IV Scene III

Sometimes, one character is not in a position to 'read' the true context, as in Sheridan's *The School for Scandal* (Act IV Scene III): Sir Peter Teazle begins, 'Well now we are alone—there *is* a Subject—my dear—Friend—on which I wish to unburthen my Mind to you . . .'. That 'subject', of course, is Lady Teazle who is in the same room, hidden by Joseph Surface behind his screen.

And in Shakespeare's *Twelfth Night* (Act III Scene IV), poor Malvolio's 'Sweet lady, ho ho' springs from a complete misreading (both literally and metaphorically!) of the situation.

Shylock thinks that in his fellow Jew, Tubal, he can for a while seek the succour of a like mind, but Tubal plays a cruel game with him, and Shylock cannot cope with the ambivalence of his intentions:

TUBAL: Yes other men have ill-luck too,—Antonio (as I heard in Genoa)—
SHYLOCK: What, what, what? ill luck, ill luck?

TUBAL: —hath an argosy cast away coming from Tripolis.
SHYLOCK: I thank God, I thank God! is it true, is it true?
TUBAL: I spoke with some of the sailors that escaped the wrack.
SHYLOCK: I thank thee, good Tubal, good news, good news: ha ha! heard in Genoa!
TUBAL: Your daughter spent in Genoa, as I heard, one night, fourscore ducats.
SHYLOCK: Thou stick'st a dagger in me,—I shall never see my gold again,—fourscore ducats at a sitting, fourscore ducats!
TUBAL: There came divers of Antonio's creditors in my company to Venice, that swear, he cannot choose but break.
SHYLOCK: I am very glad of it,—I'll plague him, I'll torture him,—I am glad of it.
TUBAL: One of them showed me a ring that he had of your daughter for a monkey.
SHYLOCK: Out upon her!—thou torturest me, Tubal,—it was my turquoise, I had it of Leah when I was a bachelor: I would not have given it for a wilderness of monkeys.
TUBAL: But Antonio is certainly undone.

Shakespeare, *The Merchant of Venice* Act III Scene I

What is the responsibility of the actors?

In a theatre there are two social contexts. The 'real' one involves an unspoken contract between members of the audience, the actors and the stage staff to share a play together. Just like any other social event it is vulnerable (if a member of the audience or an actor faints, for example). The second social situation is the fictitious event on stage.

As I said above (p. 6), most scenes in the early part of a play convey an established, on-going social event, where the characters are not consciously having to 'work at' keeping the event going. One of the techniques of acting involves the actors giving the impression that their characters are in the middle of something, when in fact the curtain went up just two minutes before. The actors use the rehearsals to 'own' the characters and to practise techniques that are *descriptive*, that is to do with deftly conveying who they are to an audience, giving the impression that life existed before the curtain went up, and giving sufficient clues to the audience through the early dialogue about the beginnings of a plot. The actor relies heavily on a number of '**givens**': information about the character, his/her relationship to other characters, the lines to be spoken, the story to get across, and where s/he should be on stage at any one time. These bind the actor to mimesis, to *imitation.* From early rehearsals through all the performances these 'givens' remain unchanged; they are *repeatable,* and s/he uses the same actions every night. His/her responsibility is to show these actions clearly to an audience, giving the impression that they are fresh. S/he is saying to the audience, 'This is how it is'; his/her actions are *adjectival.* The way s/he kisses his/her fellow actor in the early part of the play is *describing* to the audience something about the relationship between those two characters. S/he imitates this at each performance once s/he feels s/he has got it 'just right'.

I am attempting to define one extreme form of stage-acting behaviour, that is that in which the actor uses rehearsed techniques to demonstrate a feeling, a personality or a relationship (**descriptive mode**). At the other extreme there is a form of stage-acting behaviour that is close to what I described earlier (p. 4), in connection with 'real-life' situations (**existential mode**). Here there is a sufficient degree of submission to an event and a sufficient sense of living in the 'here and now', such that the participant has the feeling of making things happen as s/he goes from moment to moment. I say *close to,* for on stage such a degree of freedom is heavily qualified by the various 'givens' listed above and the responsibility to 'describe' to an audience. The tired metaphor of 'two sides of the same coin' may apply to acting on stage. If so, it is a 'loaded' coin, for the descriptive 'face' is unevenly counterbalanced by the spontaneous 'face' – lack of opportunity to change the words, change the actions, change the stage positions, change the costume, etc. often weigh heavily against living the existential moment. Any feeling of living from moment to moment may arise from an audience's response, which may or may not in turn trigger something spontaneous between the actors.

A good actor, however, will find moments of genuinely 'making something happen' even after many performances, because s/he allows him/herself to 'live' sufficiently 'inside' the event. Even something as fleeting as a new way of saying a line can throw fresh insight into a scene. This is enriching, making the actors feel 'alive', 'living' in the existential moment. It is often the case that the audience, too, senses that something very special is happening. It is doubtful, however, whether such moments occur during the years of Agatha Christie's *The Mousetrap* performances, and even a relatively short-run play of greater depth can become mechanical, with the actors depending almost entirely on 'descriptive' and 'imitative' techniques. I remember a director, dissatisfied with the deadness of performances of Shakespeare's *Hamlet* by the end of the first week's run, whispering to the actor playing the ghost to enter the stage during the battlement scene from the opposite side to that rehearsed. Did those actors become alive!

Pictorially a stage performance might look as follows. Notice that the actors on stage are almost entirely black – just a glimpse of existential experiencing within the 'showing' behaviour. The theatre audience, of course, is not showing anything, just 'submitting' themselves to the entertainment.

A stage performance

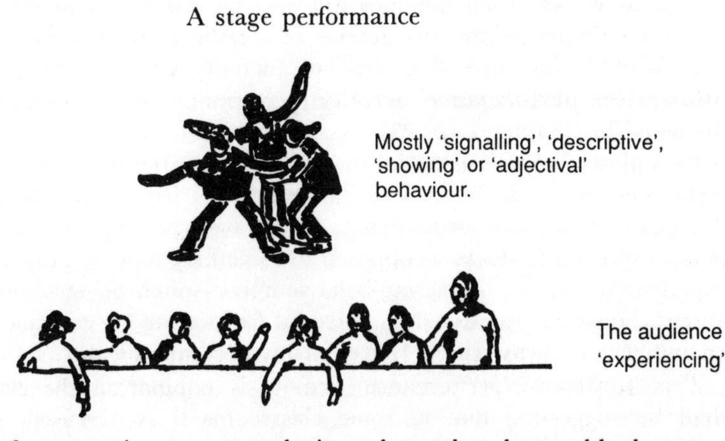

Moments of spontaneity can occur during rehearsals, when suddenly something seems 'real' to the actors, when there is a sense of 'it is happening now'. In subsequent rehearsals those existential occurrences cannot be replayed; they have to be *recalled* and *crafted* into a new 'given', and shaped into a new feature to be *described* to the potential audience. *It is an important feature of existential occurrences that they cannot be repeated.* The actor's craft lies in his ability to recall and reshape these occasional moments of spontaneity into a communicable form. (Notice that it is *not* part of the actor's craft to 'work at' a social context as participants in 'real-life' situations do, this is the playwright's responsibility. As discussed above (p. 6), the dramatist uses dialogue and specified actions to establish such contexts for the audience; to the actor, this is merely one of the 'givens'.) It is the professional actor's learned craft to be able both to 'describe' *and* 'live spontaneously' within the imitative constraints.

Amateur actors, particularly school children, sometimes fail to make the play sufficiently their own. They are so busy in a performance communicating to an audience what they have rehearsed, that this huge 'given' precludes their finding a truly spontaneous interaction with fellow actors and audience. Sometimes one sees child performers thrown by an audience that behaves differently from the previous night's audience.

Drama in the classroom

I have so far used words like 'descriptive', 'adjectival', 'showing', 'communicating' and 'repeatable' as a means of conveying those qualities characterising Theatre Performance (using capital letters to distinguish from classroom performance). These characteristics, heavily dependent on imitation, are acquired after many hours of rehearsal, perhaps over a period of several weeks. Such qualities are also on *instant* tap in the classroom – a pupil might imitate the actions of a policeman or a snooker player. This kind of 'instant coffee' dramatic activity might usefully be termed **'illustrative/performance' activity** (performance with a small p). This is discussed in Chapter 2 (p. 23).

This phrase implies a 'given' that is being referred to; it allows the actor to be seen as a vehicle for a narrative or plot; it suggests showing something; and it implies an audience. 'Illustrative/performance' activity also implies something *shown*, as opposed to something *occurring*, the 'existential/experiential' side of the acting-behaviour coin often being almost entirely absent. However, the dynamic potential for making an exciting impact on an audience is always there. It is descriptive, communicable, and repetitive.

This 'illustrative/performance' activity is popular in the classroom. I shall be suggesting that in some classrooms it is overused, that some children's dramatic experience is confined to such audience-centred acting behaviour. Nevertheless, it is a powerful dramatic tool and it is discussed in detail in Chapter 4.

I have also used an alternative set of words and phrases, like 'existential', 'submitting', 'spontaneous' and 'here-and-now', to convey those qualities which, while only intermittently and minimally evident in stage-acting, are critical to experiencing social events. I am interested in how these qualities may also be harnessed to dramatic activity in the classroom. They are to be found in a form of dramatic activity I term **dramatic playing** which, as you will see, combines descriptive and existential behaviour. Such an activity I recommend should be adopted for 90 per cent of young children's drama and should never entirely disappear from the drama work of adolescents. I believe that, for young children in particular, it provides the basis for effective learning, and gives them the ground rules of dramatic art. It also helps adolescents to seek the dynamic existential quality in their Performance (with a capital P) of the school play.

To summarise, I believe there are three ways of helping children and students to 'make meaning' using enactment. One is through the long process of rehearsal leading to Performance, which obviously cannot be part of classroom practice. The second is to use the illustrative/performance activity, the many forms of which are discussed in Chapter 4. The third, perhaps the most powerful, is to use the dramatic playing activity examined in detail in Chapter 2.

2 Two Kinds of Dramatic Activity in Classroom Drama

The dramatic playing activity: the intention to 'make' a social context – in which interesting things can happen

In the dramatic playing activity (Davis & Lawrence, 1986) the participants draw on the social context-making skills we use in 'real-life' situations. These were discussed in Chapter 1 (p. 2). Just as in 'life situations' we 'work at' our social contexts to make them believable to ourselves, so it is in 'dramatic playing'; just as in 'life situations' we initially describe to each other the kind of situation it is, so it is in 'dramatic playing'; just as in 'life situations' such events are fragile, so it is in 'dramatic playing'; just as in 'life situations' the participants need to *submit* to and trust the situation in order to experience it, so it is in 'dramatic playing'; just as in 'real life' participants may be relatively active or passive within the situation, so it is in 'dramatic playing; just as in 'real life' participants operate spontaneously in the 'here and now', so it is in dramatic playing. *One critical difference is that, although in 'real life' we may only be conscious of 'working at' a social context when something goes wrong, in dramatic playing one is constantly aware of the effort required.* Indeed, the power and the *fun* of the experience stem from fully recognising that one is in two social contexts at the same time. One has a dual perception of the world, what Augusto Boal (1979) calls 'metaxis'. There is the world around of fellow players agreeing to make believe, and the fictitious world of the 'play' – the thing created. The participants creating their dramatic fiction experience a tension, a feeling that something special is going on, that something *must happen* because they have elected or contracted to make it happen. I call this the **imperative tension**.

After the initial 'demonstrating', signalling what the context is, the mode of behaviour is that of spontaneous interaction which is minimally dependent on mimesis. Although there is always something from 'the world out there' as a point of reference (for example 'Let's play bank robbers' is likely to be sustained by appropriate 'bank robber' behaviour), the potential richness of the experience lies in its fluidity. 'The thing created' is *newly* created existentially from moment to moment. Nor do the participants see what they are creating as something repeatable. They may finally say, 'Let's do "bank-robbers" again', but not with a view to copying what they did before, just as one might say after a successful party, 'We must do it again'.

This being freed from the need to see the creation as repeatable is a significant feature. It is one of the characteristics that distinguishes 'dramatic playing' activity from what the actor does in rehearsal, or what children do if sent into small groups for ten minutes to make up a play to show to the rest of the class when the time is up. Both the actor and the small-group performers, as they explore, do so in terms of credibility, repeatability and communicability. They do not allow themselves the luxury of an existential experience, for even as they enter the experience they immediately qualify it, because they know its purpose is to show it later to someone else.

I have observed children from Infant School to Comprehensive, from Kindergarten to Senior High, whose diet of drama has *excluded* the possibility of dramatic playing. Their drama work has *always* been seen in terms of its repeatabilility and communicability to an audience. Indeed, whenever I read a theoretical writer in the field of the Arts who emphasises drama as a 'performing' art, I wonder whether such a theorist is, by implication, denying the opportunity for an existential experience within dramatic playing. Because this form of dramatic activity harnesses those very processes that we go through when we make social contexts in 'real life', I believe it creates a unique opportunity for the participants to reflect on the meaning of what they are creating. Because it relies minimally on mimesis, the participant is *living* the event rather than just *copying* it. What does 'dramatic playing' activity look like in practice?

Imagine groups of Puritan parents interrogating their daughters about 'what occurred in Salem woods last night'; corrupt town councillors holding a public meeting in which they have to cover up vested interests; treasure-hunters poring over a map of an island for clues; monks trying to find out who the stranger is who has sought sanctuary; Normans designing an impregnable castle; the staff of the King's palace making preparations for the new princess's christening; neighbours advising Red Riding Hood's mother she should not let her daughter go off into the woods on her own, even if her grandmother does live on the other side!; and so on. I have just taken illustrations randomly from my own teaching. Notice that in order to give a thumbnail sketch for the reader there is an implied tension, which, of course, is discussed later, but there is also in each case a defined social context.

This social context is the prime responsibility of the participants. If they fail to 'make' such a context, then the drama cannot work. Whereas in a play Performance the context has to be credible to an audience, in the case of dramatic playing it has to be credible to the participants, as in 'real life'. In 'life situations' the event or context has to be believable to the *participants*, not to some hypothetical audience. It must meet the participants' notion of 'how it has to be'. The particpants' collective knowledge of such an event may be very crude, but it will still have its own rules which the participants will need to abide by if it is to be believable to them. Thus the criterion of *logic* appertains. Problems arise if some participants 'know better' than others what the implicit rules are. Suppose some of the Puritan daughters (in the example above) simply behaved like outspoken adolescents, nearer to a twentieth-century than a seventeenth-century style, the drama would collapse because it would lack credibility in the eyes of others. On such an occasion a teacher might wish to step in and do some teaching. Even if none of the participants seem to appreciate the Puritan code of family conduct, the teacher (knowing better!) may feel it is something the group *ought* to give attention to if they are to get anything out of the scene. Thus, in this instance, a 'given from the world out there' overrides tolerance of inaccurate representation, and imitation necessarily takes over. (If, on the other hand, the class comprised low-achievers with special needs doing drama for the first time, the teacher is unlikely to intervene with *his/her* sense of logic). The chance to 'live in the here and now' is still there for the participants, however, within the new set of rules. Indeed, there is an increased chance of creative exploration *because* of the greater strictures.

The extent to which 'the world out there' needs to be represented is not always a straightforward matter. Sometimes, for the sake of 'building belief', it is imperative that there is some kind of sign, either through an object or through action, of an external feature of that world. For example a black-drape oblong on the floor suggests a body, a telephone indicates 'Samaritans', and a drawing of a computer represents 'office'. Meticulous miming of cracking a safe signals 'the expert' at work, standing to attention says 'guard', and miming card-playing, typing, sending Morse code, sharpening a knife, etc. are all actions that may be used to signify a particular social context. Notice that such actions or objects may not be important *in themselves* – they are simply acting as indicators, labelling the context. But even decisions about what *kind* of object or action should be used can be quite complex. Take the example of a telephone. There could be three options: miming telephoning, a drawing of a telephone and a 'real' telephone. Any one of these could be the most appropriate, depending on the nature of the play being created and the needs of the class. While under some circumstances the physical presence of a telephone on a table is needed to establish a particular place where significant two-way communication can occur, there could be times when its very physicality becomes an inhibition when, for example, possible clumsy handling of the real receiver could act *against* believability. Likewise, the *drawing* of the telephone marks the *place* as important, or the person sitting beside it as important, giving little significance to the actual action.

Having no telephone at all can be the most real, for sometimes an object can become more real by an absence of representation. Recently, when I was working with a group of adults in Salzburg, Austria, this very problem of the extent to which the use of a 'real' object becomes a stimulus or a block towards creativity manifested itself very clearly for two of the participants. I started the class off on the theme of 'Robin Hood' (discussed in detail later in Chapter 5 (p. 70)) by asking them, in pairs, simply to adopt the role of a father teaching his apprentice son how to make arrows. One particular couple looked around the room and were delighted to find in a vase some dried ferns which were thin, smooth stalks (the length of an arrow!) with 'feathery' appendages at one end. They couldn't believe their luck! But, of course, whereas *initially* such a 'prop' works for credibility, the longer the interaction is sustained the less credible the 'arrow' becomes, for the prop remains stubbornly there as a subtly persistent reminder of the ways in which it *differs* from an arrow. It is the 'arrow in the mind' that in the long run, however elusive to begin with, becomes believable. And, of course, it is not only the arrow itself that becomes 'real', the process of believing in the arrow generates the process of believing the fictitious roles. To use Vygotski's terminology (1933), the arrow becomes the 'pivot' which allows the participants to enter the medieval makebelieve. But unlike Vygotski's classic example of straddling a stick as representing riding a horse, the pivot in the Robin Hood exercise has to be 'in the head'. Even if you were able to obtain a *real* arrow for the participants to handle, this could become an even bigger block to creativity. The actors could feel *stuck* with the reality of its presence, only too painfully aware of the incompatibility of their inexperienced handling, and the legitimate context for owning such an arrow would seem even more remote.

Thus the opposite usage can sometimes be valid. The underlying principle appears to be related to the *way* in which an object is to be used. If we needed a 'sign' to say, 'this is an arrowmaker's house', then a quiver of 'dried ferns' would fulfil that function. However, if the object is to be used beyond that of indicator, if it is to become the centre of the *action* and in turn the means by which the participants are to develop belief in their individual roles, then it is sometimes more productive to rely on the 'arrow in the mind'. Paradoxically, the less familiar the context to the participants, the more likely the use of 'real' objects will be a hindrance.

Sometimes the relationship between actuality and fiction can be very complicated. In some teaching in Johannesburg of an examination class studying the Industrial Revolution in England, Dorothy Heathcote used a dramatic metaphor. This involved the death of an elderly member of the family whose memorabilia led the remaining family (the class) to discover the man's near and distant past in England, covering pre-industrial and industrial periods. An early part of the drama began with the 'family' making wreaths for the funeral. The flowers for the wreaths were to be *paper* flowers made from pink tissues, and the base for each wreath was card-board, so they were in fact 'window-dressing' wreaths, *but the class did actually make them.* These were objects that subsequently needed to be seen and used, unlike the arrows above. *As* they made them, Dorothy asked them to talk in role as members of the dead man's family. They discussed some of the problems they were facing as a result of having to arrange to spend a year in England doing research, in compliance with the dead man's will. This was the class's first experience of dramatic playing. The 'here and now' of actually making the decorative wreaths no doubt 'protected' them into finding a 'here and now' within the fiction of having a family conversation. They were then asked to write down some of the problems in the centre of their wreath, in the midst of the flowers!

The previous day they had had experience of 'directing' (a legitimate part of classroom drama which is discussed later (p. 24)). They modelled the portrait of the 'dead man' using an adult observer of the class as a 'guinea-pig'. Interestingly, a *woman* volunteered to be the portrait, once more demonstrating that the notion of drama as creating a replica of the 'world out there' is misleading. However, the woman wore vaguely mannish garments without a tie (but a tie was at hand had the class felt it appropriate). They proceeded to make all kinds of decisions about what they wanted the 'portrait' to show – by implication. Having created the portrait they then had the experience of hearing the old man's will read out in the study (the pupils' choice of room) *in front of the portrait*, so that the picture they had made became the new stimulus for another 'dramatic playing' episode. Their work on the portrait was now placed 'in context', allowing them to experience the dramatic present.

Then the mixture of fiction and actuality became even more complex! They were to attend the 'lying in' of the dead man. Each sub-family in turn was to lay its wreath at the coffin, saying a few words to the dead, combining thanks for the past and concerns for the prospect of research in England.

How did Dorothy decide to represent this? The students came into the room to find a narrow table – coffin length – in the middle. At the head was an enlarged photocopy of the 'portrait's' head and hands, with a *real* tie round the 'neck' of the photocopy. The rest of the 'body' was a black cloth. Around the body were one or two wreaths, plus written extracts from the will relating to the old man's imposition on the family. And sitting at the head of the table was the woman who had played the portrait, still wearing her 'portrait' clothes. As each family group came forward with their wreath they could, if they wished, whisper (these adolescents were very shy in the early stages of this work) their thanks and worries directly to the woman. She then formally, eloquently and publically restated, for all the room to hear, the meaning of what had been said to her.

It is unlikely that this kind of complexity will be within the repertoire of the average teacher. Indeed, it may be of some comfort to appreciate that there are occasions when it is not necessary to have 'props' of any kind. If the social context being created is not only very familiar to the participants but also emotionally charged, then there is often less need to have objects or actions signalling some external feature of that context in order to 'build belief'. Imagine a group of teachers making up a play about teachers in a staffroom. Because their necessary points of reference are so familiar to them – 'below the surface', as it were – having 'this is a staffroom' indicators would be redundant. It is worth noting that this flexibility (of deciding to what extent external features of a context should remain 'in the mind') is not available to the same extent when a play is being performed to an audience. For the audience a real telephone, something resembling a real quiver of arrows, a coffin or a portrait is usually (although not always) necessary.

Notice that in earlier paragraphs I slipped into using words like 'indicating' and 'signalling'. It is useful here to remind yourself of what was established in Chapter 1: that in 'real-life' social contexts we *initially* adopt 'descriptive' behaviour in order to signal to each other what kind of social event we are in. The same applies to 'dramatic playing' activity. Just as in everyday life the interviewer indicates what kind of interview it is to be by choosing to sit formally behind his/her desk rather than placing drinks glasses by the easy chairs, so in 'dramatic playing' the same thing occurs. Only when the social context is *established* can the descriptive behaviours yield to the more spontaneous interactive behaviour of the existential mode. To reiterate an important point made earlier (p. 11), just as in 'real life' if something goes wrong, so that credibility is threatened and descriptive behaviours are quickly resumed by the participants, so, too, if a drama experience starts to lose credibility – it often occurs when a participant behaves in a way the others see as illogical – the responsibility lies with the group to re-signal what the situation is. Thus dramatic playing activity is normally made up of two phases: the descriptive and the existential. If the latter is threatened the descriptive will again take over until the disturbance is eliminated. Pictorially, 'dramatic playing' activity follows the same sequence as shown earlier (p. 5) for 'real-life' situations.

Below is a repeat of the figures on p. 5, but this time they represent not a 'real-life' social context but a fictitious context created through 'dramatic playing' activity, and taking place in a classroom. The sequence remains exactly the same as for real life.

Sometimes the 'descriptive' occurs in 'real life' and 'dramatic playing' activity, not because something has gone wrong but because one or more of the participants takes on the responsibility of reporting something that has happened. I call this the 'narrative voice'.

The 'narrative voice' within 'dramatic playing'

Bruner (1990) discussed the findings of research into the considerable extent to which four to five-year old children adopt a **narrative form** of discourse. He suggests that this common form of communication has deep implications for the child's development in 'meaning-making'. It gives the child power over past events; it is the child's way of absorbing the 'canons' of cultural behaviour; it may well reconcile, justify or excuse, but these are not its primary purpose, which is to *explicate* the past experience.

It would be interesting to conduct research into many different kinds of adult social contexts, for it is my experience that adoption of the narrative form dominates most social interaction – most of our 'talk' is in the past tense. (I could never understand why, when I was taught languages at school, the early emphasis was always on the present tense.) There are a fair number of social contexts when it is legitimate for one member of the group to *narrate* something to the others. Such a 'narrator' adopts a public mode of 'describing' something to an 'audience'. Brecht's 'Street Accident' (1964) is a classic example of what I mean.

Not surprisingly this narration also features commonly in dramatic playing activity. An examination of the dialogue of typical interaction in a drama will reveal that a great deal of *relating* what has happened goes on *within* the drama. This is not just stylistic ornamentation, it is absolutely vital to the 'meaning-making' processes. This form of reflection within the fiction itself is an explication of experience.

'Dramatic playing' as theatre

'Building belief' is an early hurdle in any makebelieve playing, but there are other responsibilities that emerge if the work is to be worthwhile. Although dramatic playing activity draws on those descriptive and existential qualities of behaviour to be found in 'real-life' social situations, such qualities alone do not *define* dramatic playing. I have already shown, for instance, that all drama is dependent on the participants having a dual awareness of both the 'real' and the 'fictitious' worlds. You will further see that the aesthetic dimension is also a defining attribute. This brings me to *a central thesis of this book.*

Making fictitious social events is a form of makebelieve playing, but it only becomes significant as *dramatic art* when attention is given to the art form of theatre. This attention may be the teacher's, the participants' or both. The teacher may set up the experience in such a way that the participants *experience* theatre without their realising it, or the participants may consciously contrive to create theatre as they make the social event believable to themselves. Occasionally a theatrical element is employed by the participants without their giving it conscious attention. The 'imperative tension' creating the feeling that something important is going to happen can drive a group towards a sustained piece of makebelieve that can be all-absorbing. I recently witnessed a very talented class of mature students at New York University engage in such an experience for over 20 minutes. In this instance there were 28 adults all weaving a medieval social context with a total sense of commitment. Because the theatrical elements were not clearly defined it was almost impossible to follow what was happening – but *they* knew! In retrospect one could isolate the theatrical elements of 'deception', 'constraint', 'withholding the truth', etc., but the participants themselves were barely aware of them for they were wrapped up in 'living' within what they found to be an enriching context. I as teacher, redundant, simply watched from the side-line. But this kind of achievement from adults is rare (this was an exceptional class). More often than not there is a conscious striving towards artistic form in successful drama. I shall now look more closely at what this implies.

There is a fundamental sense in which art copies life. Artists are aware that in life we enjoy and give significance to *relationships* between things – we have a capacity for finding significance in order and disorder, harmony and discord, resolution and irresolution, the expected and unexpected, sameness and difference, repetition, etc. The way sounds, shapes, colours, actions and words relate to each other is often significant.

This is the *aesthetic* dimension that can be observed in many social events in 'real-life' situations. Everyday we consciously set out to give significance and a sense of order to our social contexts by paying attention to our use of space, time, sequence, uniformity, colour and hierarchy. In other words, instead of the stature of an event being self-explanatory, the *form* of the event implies this importance. The positioning of a judge's chair, a monarch's throne, a chieftain's tepee or a church altar are obvious examples of the significant use of space. The agreed choice of words and music, and their sequence in the liturgy, attends to the significant use of sound. The use of style and colour in garments worn at military, political and ecclesiastical ceremonies is yet another way of giving significance to an event. One could go on endlessly down to a simple ritualistic gesture such as a handshake. All these are examples of an aesthetic dimension, that is *where the meaning of the event is, at least partially, encapsulated in its form.* It seems to be a basic human urge to bring order to social activities by investing the meaning of the activity within its form.

Artists apply this use of form from everyday life to their art. Form in art is not something special to art, it is simply that the artist uses these 'everyday' aesthetic dimensions. This is nowhere more apparent than in drama, where the devices the dramatist/actor uses on stage are those we use in 'real life'. But in drama it is not just the *ritualised* events of life that the artist copies, for s/he draws on all those kinds of moments that in everyday life we would call 'dramatic', that is when something has surprised us, when there is a 'tense' moment, when something *must* happen, when temporary chaos is created because a ritual has been broken or when we are made aware of the manipulation of time or space. For example, in connection with the latter case, imagine an authority figure who requires us to walk across the room to his desk (he is manipulating space) where he keeps us standing. Then he allows a silence to fall before answering our request (he is manipulating time). In both of these examples the authority figure is using *form* to enhance the meaning of the situation.

Teacher and dramatist thus have at least two kinds of *formal* dimension at their disposal: the ordering (and breaking) of experience associated with the formalities of ritual, ceremony or procedure; and the enhancement of experience that arises from effective use of imperative tension, contrast, surprise, constraint and repetition within moment-to-moment interaction between the characters. A third dimension is also available – the aesthetic quality of the dialogue itself. Recently I was teaching in a Senior High School in New Jersey where the class (Grades 9 and 11) and I slipped into high-level formal language as we created a drama about searching for the Holy Grail. The language dominated the action and it became apparent to us that the few gestures that were needed had to match the formality of the language. None of these formal dimensions, however, can operate without the imperative tension that gives the makebelieve its dynamic, the feeling that something important must happen.

I argued earlier in this chapter (p. 11) that participants in 'dramatic playing' are 'working at' making a social context or event, just as we are doing all the time (perhaps without realising it) in 'real life'. The principal resource is one of *logic*: they have to recognise the implicit rules of the context and know how to apply them, and to experience the context fully they have to be prepared to 'give themselves' existentially to it. Such a description might be sufficient to account for some 'dramatic playing' that occurs in children's makebelieve play. However, for the activity to qualify as an *art form* it should be characterised by a *formal element* of some kind, for it is only theatre when attention is given to an aesthetic dimension that, at least in part, carries the meaning of the experience.

I had better pause here to discuss the way I am using the term 'theatre'. Terminology is so confusing, and I may well be guilty of making it more so! By 'theatre' I mean when the art form is working for the participants (or for an audience), when something is happening in the classroom or on stage that to some degree 'takes over' the participants or the audience, when the meanings of what they are creating or watching resonate beyond the literal meaning of their actions and words. Theatre is something bigger than the people making it. I hope this doesn't sound too 'gooey'. If it does, then substitute 'dramatic art form' in your mind whenever I use 'theatre'.

The most obvious way of achieving a sense of form in dramatic playing is to copy those rituals, ceremonies and procedures that enhance our everyday experience. Thus a classroom drama with actions that copy courtroom procedure, soldiers on guard, a 'swearing in' ceremony, graduation, school assembly, a wedding, reading a will, standing at a grave-side, interview procedure, proposing a toast, or any event where there is a proper way of *ordering* things, has a greater chance of making the drama seem significant. I have already given an example of this kind of formality in Dorothy Heathcote's Johannesburg teaching, when the pupils in turn placed their wreaths by the coffin. The use of this kind of formal dimension goes some way towards dramatic art. The easily identifiable forms of ceremony, ritual and procedure contribute to 'building belief', for there is nothing quite like, 'Will the court be upstanding', to make you feel that you are there! But more than this is required if the participants are to be working as *artists* in their chosen medium.

While we have established that there is a basic connection between making a 'real-life' social event and making such an event in makebelieve, there must also be a sense of *using form* to make ordinary events significant. For instance if you picture the following examples of dramatic playing among children of various ages, the existential mode in each case is enhanced by the apparent attention to form.

> The stranger at the sanctuary door is obliged to hammer three times before the monks, at compline prayers, rise to let the stranger in; it is a metallic intrusion on their silence.
>
> From the edge of the room the people view the 'mystery box that no one must touch' standing on a table in the middle.
>
> When the two pieces of charred paper are put together, the scrawled message reads, 'h.e.l.p . . . m.e.'.
>
> The group move slowly in their anger towards the huddled figure in the far corner.

These examples are so obvious that they are hardly worth discussing, but it is in my experience that teachers and students are not always alert to these aesthetic possibilities. For instance let us take the first example where sound and silence were used effectively. A group, whose members were ignorant of the potential of such theatrical elements, might casually have the stranger arrive during supper – one knock and he's in! Placing it in a context where there is already a strong sense of order and no talking, and additionally having the knocking breaking the silence three times, enhances the significance of the stranger's arrival, symbolising the intrusion. What is also of interest is to know whether it was *planned* this way (in this instance from my own teaching it *was* planned) or whether in the ongoing situation it felt right to the participants to wait until the third knock. When it thus happens spontaneously it is an indicator that the group are, in the very best sense, '*working in theatre*'. They are enjoying a sense of form and understand the means of achieving it.

In the second example the group used the distance from the box to enhance the box's mystery. The third example used a carefully focused sort of dramatic problem-solving and surprise to start an adventure. The fourth group, more sophisticated, recognised that rushing over in anger to a victim may be true to 'real life', but working in theatre more effectively requires the slow covering of space between the tight-knit group and the isolated figure.

This application of theatre form *occurs* within the existential experience. This seems to be a concept that many theorists in drama education and writers of arts-project publications find very difficult to grasp, so difficult they often ignore it! Sometimes, however, they may respond with, 'So what? Surely all actors use these elements of theatre, particularly the manipulation of time, space and tension, etc. in their acting?'. Of course they are right, actors *do* use such techniques, but such observations miss the point that I am making. This is that as drama educators we should, first and foremost, be concerned with helping our groups of pupils to see theatre as an *ensemble* creation, requiring ensemble techniques that provide the *base-line* for the dramatic art form. Such a base-line will eventually provide the resources for an individual's acting ability, but it is the ensemble thinking, seeing and hearing that must come first if we are to educate all of our pupils in the art of drama. Teacher-educators in drama, alas, seem to fail to give this base-line sufficient attention. It is not surprising, therefore, that teachers themselves often feel inadequate in helping their pupils to find theatre in the existential aspect of dramatic playing. Interestingly, teachers, pupils and drama-education theorists are more ready to recognise theatre form in the alternative to dramatic playing – the illustrative/performance activity of classroom drama.

The 'illustrative performance' activity: the intention to show an idea

This form of classroom drama is just as important, in both educational and artistic terms, as dramatic playing, but it should be used sparingly with young children. They need the foundation offered by the existential experiencing and, for them, too much early emphasis on credibility, repeatability and communicability to an audience can be damaging. By its very nature the illustrative/performance activity relies on what things and people look like *from the outside*. I shudder when I watch young children who are trained as part of their drama programme to *show* emotions at the drop of a hat!: 'Show us a happy boy', 'a sad girl', 'an angry person', etc. This is imitation at its worst. Such pupils never have the chance of 'dramatic playing', and if they did they would be unlikely to have a true experience because they would be too busy considering 'how it looks'. So, in offering our pupils 'illustrative/performance', we must make sure they grasp the distinction between the two modes. The illustrative/performance activity is indeed like 'instant coffee', although this does not do justice to the excitement that can be felt by both creators and audience when it is at its best. 'Dramatic playing' at its best, when it is operating truthfully using theatrical elements to do so, begins as 'instant coffee' and merges into 'real coffee'. What occurs in a theatre between well-rehearsed actors and an audience is, of course, also 'real coffee'. (One of my New York University students suggested rehearsals without the presence of an audience could be described as decaffeinated!) This 'coffee' metaphor should not be taken too seriously, but it is certainly its *instant* quality that characterises the 'illustrative' activity. This is both its strength and its weakness. It has an over-dependence on imitation but the advantage of immediate feedback and, as you will see, if handled properly it places a responsibility on the rest of the class as audience. Because of its function as a stimulus for ideas and its precision of form, it leads to productive thinking. It can also be powerfully moving and entertaining.

The simplest example of the illustrative/performance activity is the use of '**tableau**' – sculpture, photograph, still picture or still depiction (terminology that implies the differing complexity of the task). This usually entails pupils getting into small groups, discussing a focus, trying things out to meet the task, holding the picture still while the rest of the class observes, relaxing and hearing comments, and giving further explanation if it seems necessary. Such an exercise is commonplace in drama classes, but often the richness of educational opportunities in such an exercise is overlooked. It is worth giving some detailed attention to it, as much of what I say here applies to the many more complex, more sophisticated extensions of the exercise.

I will here draw attention to some of the inherent values of 'tableau':

1 That it is small-group work and that the techniques (*still* picture) are simplified to instant showing, whatever the subject matter is, makes it more controllable. Because its simplicity is likely to generate confidence, pupils will become more adventuresome in their use of subtleties as they realise the potential in the material. For instance moving from a 'straight' photograph showing family hierarchy to showing family affections or tensions, and further to 'disguised' family tensions! In addition they may go through a process of selecting, rejecting and accepting, and modifying ideas and their interpretations. The exercise requires imagination and discipline. It is a truly creative process, *and yet* the goal is relatively accessible.

2 The 'showing' stage is itself of value. It is useful to the small group to have its ideas confirmed or questioned by the class, but it also provides an opportunity for the other members of the class to see themselves as active observers, with a responsibility for interpretation and the furtherance of ideas. (Indeed, an alternative approach is to have the rest of the class operating as *directors* by having them direct the small group as guinea-pig actors in the first place). The *way* in which the class discusses its interpretation of what it is audience to should guarantee an *active* audience that is *challenged* by what has been created for it. This shift, from the small group's participation in a depiction to an audience's role in using what has been created for its own enlightenment and as a stimulus to new work, is to make full use of this exercise.

3 The most valuable aspects of this kind of depiction lie in the often astonishing effect that can be achieved in a relatively short space of time. If the task moves beyond 'photograph' to, say, 'an abstract sculpture', then there is considerable potential for getting to the heart of the subject matter. So, for instance, if it is a chapter of a novel, a poem, or a character, the participants can often find subtle ways to convey its *essence*. It is often the case, too, that this kind of task stimulates high-quality discussion in the group during the preparation of its sculpture.

4 Although the technical requirement is purely descriptive – 'instant coffee'! – there are many occasions when such is the power of the product created by adolescents and older participants that, at the moment of sharing it with an audience, the classroom becomes alive with a feeling of recognition, revelation and awe that belongs to 'real coffee'. It is only momentary, of course, but the power of the exercise lies in its

capacity to produce for a few seconds that very quality that professional actors work to achieve for the length of a play performance.

There are other ways of using the illustrative/performance dramatic activity. I have already mentioned having the class as directors, using a small group as actor guinea-pigs. When I first started to teach drama, any occasion when a small group was brought out to the front carried the implication that the 'success' of the exercise rested on the talents of the 'actors'. Any subsequent discussion centred on 'how well so-and-so acted his/her part'. In the usage I am now suggesting its success is dependent on the imagination of the 'directors', for the 'actors' may simply be offering themselves for manipulation, merely carrying out the directors' instructions using appropriate 'descriptive' technique. The directors will use their understanding of theatrical elements, especially the manipulation of space. Students must learn that bodies on a stage make a statement.

The whole emphasis of this work is on *substance*, what the illustrations have to say. The pupils are always concerned with being quite clear as to *what* they want to illustrate. Their understanding is not static, for new things will be learnt as they discuss an idea for, say, a sculpture, and, importantly, new understandings emerge from the sculpture itself. This is a far remove from the traditional 'Go into your corners to make up a play', although, of course, this will sometimes have its place.

Perhaps the most elaborate form of this illustrative/performance work is **Forum Theatre**, as propounded by Augusto Boal (1979). I enjoy using this form in the classroom, but I have also seen some seriously watered-down versions. It is important to remember that you should only do Forum Theatre if the audience has a *vested interest in the problem.* For instance you would be pretty safe in a school situation dealing with the topic of school discipline, but do not attempt to use Forum Theatre where the posed problem is of intellectual interest only to your class.

Although Forum Theatre 'proper' is dependent on a group of actors having prepared and pre-rehearsed a scene for an audience, it is possible in the classroom to use a simpler, but nevertheless effective, version (simpler in *form* that is, not in substance!). The method merely involves asking two people to enact a short incident – perhaps just a single line of dialogue – where the first actor is 'oppressed' by the other. This is a good example of illustrative/performance activity, for the actors are simply demonstrating an idea. The theme might be sexual harassment, racism, parent's manipulation of an offspring, the offspring's maipulation of a parent, etc. The class is first invited to confirm the credibility of the performance, and then to attempt to show, by taking the place of the first actor, how the victim might throw off the oppression. As there is always the danger of stereotype or unrealistic solutions in dealing with this kind of issue, the teacher sees this work as simply an *introduction* to a theme whose complexity is to be explored subsequently, using many different angles and many different drama forms, including the dramatic playing. The importance of teacher planning in terms of a *sequence* of experience is dealt with in Chapter 5 (p. 65).

Another extension of the illustrative/performance activity which can be very effective with older adolescents and adults is **Chamber Theatre**, where an extract from a novel is closely examined and, by using a range of narratorial 'voices', the actual lines of the script (not necessarily in a dialogue form) can be performed. I understand the North American use of Story Theatre can also be effective, although this is not something I have tried. Again, a simpler version of this work, particularly useful in the close examination of play-texts, is to use 'alter egos'. Alternatively a variety of narrative devices can be used: one actor as narrator; two actors sharing the narration; or two narrators, one giving the hidden thoughts of the characters while the other gives the audience background information of a social, political or historical nature relating to the scene as a whole.

These devices are not merely a way of extending the teacher's repertoire, they are a necessary part of using illustrative/performance activity. The form is but 'instant coffee', and there is little chance that an actor can show the kind of depth of character one would expect of an actor after several rehearsals. Thus, because an actor using this mode is limited in the kind of statement s/he can make about his/her role, pupils and teacher must seek as many different means as possible, such as the use of narrative or 'alter ego', of making the inner feelings, the subtext, the implications, the explanations, etc. accessible to the rest of the class. It is only by engaging with these hidden things that a class will really learn. The responsibility for making the implicit explicit may lie either with the small group of actors or with the rest of the class as directors. And, of course, what they discover is that introducing ploys such as 'alter ego' or 'narrator' makes exciting theatre in itself. It is interesting to note the number of modern plays that have experimented with both of these devices. Although I realise that adolescents need to be given *some* experience of naturalistic theatre, I actually encourage my own classes to embrace abstract or stylised theatre, where they can experiment with a variety of forms to convey many layers of meaning.

Mime in its simplest form is an example of illustrative/performance activity. To have Mime without an audience (I am differentiating Mime from *miming actions* as a regular feature of 'dramatic playing') is pointless. In essence all this is saying is, 'This is how it is done'. Unfortunately, because it can be so simple, many teachers assume it is suitable for young children. Generally speaking this is a form of mimesis that leads to relatively little learning, for showing how actions are done is not something even young children need to have explained. The art form of Mime is, of course, in a different category altogether, conveying sophisticated meanings through its art. But there is an in-between form that is worth trying with adolescents in particular – using *narration* or *alter ego* during the mime actions. This again is a way of bringing depth to the 'illustrative/performance' drama.

This may seem to be turning out to be an arbitrary list, but by giving names to a few forms I am trying to encourage flexibility. Teacher and pupils together can invent a form that simply feels right for what they are trying to explore. There must be nearly as many ways of using the illustrative/performance form as there are of engaging in dramatic playing. Pictorially, it is nicely contrasted with dramatic playing activity (Figures A & B, p. 5), as follows. Notice hints of white among the black of this 'demonstrating an idea' activity. The 'spectators' of his classroom work are, of course, the rest of the class – *actively* engaged in the work, but as directors not performers.

The 'illustractive/performance' activity

'Showing', 'descriptive', 'demonstrating', 'repeatable'

'Active' audience or directors

I have drawn a distinction then between two forms of dramatic activity. The most straightforward is illustrative/performance activity. This is because it is characterised by just one mode of acting behaviour, that of 'describing', showing' or 'demonstrating'. Usually it illustrates an idea (or ideas) – the actors' own, or those of the audience, the members of which often operate as directors.

The dramatic playing activity, on the other hand, is more complicated, for the purpose here is to create a social context and, like all social contexts, it is characterised by a mixture of descriptive and existential behaviours. There is a time-sequence dimension here related to the initial and subsequent stages. It has been pointed out that when something goes wrong a retreat to 'descriptive' behaviours often occurs. At other times 'descriptive behaviours' occur when one of the participants adopts a 'narrative voice'.

It is probably not possible to conceive of either descriptive or existential modes in their purest form, that the seeds of the one are always present in the other. Sometimes it is possible to have a 'mini-performance', using the descriptive, demonstrating mode within the existential mode. In some respects this is not too different from the use of 'narrative voice'.

'Demonstrating an idea' within the 'dramatic playing' activity

More explicitly descriptive than 'narrative' within dramatic playing is the use of *illustrative/performance action* by the participants. This occurs when the pupils 'in role' switch to showing each other an idea. Thus, for instance, when I set up a drama in which the students were all trainee journalists, in discussing techniques of interviewing witnesses in order to get a good story out of them we switched to asking one 'journalist' to 'play the role' of the 'interviewer', and the other 'journalist' to be the 'witness'. They proceeded to *demonstrate* their (and our) ideas on how to get the most out of the witness. This is like a play within a play. Whereas in the latter case the acting behaviour is existential, within the former a descriptive mode is adopted.

The distinction between the two modes is not always so clear-cut. Sometimes it is difficult to discern which mode is operating, just as in real life it is not always easy to distinguish between working hard to get things going and submitting to the occasion (and vice versa). I have mentioned (p. 4) the possibility of something going wrong in a way that causes the participants to revert to descriptive signalling in order to reconfirm the social context, but sometimes it is the *teacher* who deliberately interferes with the existential flow with a view to challenging the group. Such an example of teacher intervention occurred when I worked with a group of fifteen/sixteen-year olds on the text of Pinter's *The Room*, as described here.

I had set up a sustained improvisational scene relating to a group of people visiting a strange, out-of-the-way boarding house run by a mysterious old man (me!). The dramatic playing activity moved quickly with these experienced students into the existential mode, but my view of what was occurring was guided by two concerns: the danger that the activity was becoming too much like formless 'free-playing', and that the purpose of the exercise was to take the class close to the atmosphere of Pinter's script. In my role I behaved as if I were trying to hide monstrous secrets; they in turn quite rightly set out to challenge me. But it lacked theatre form so, once they were well-established in their dramatic 'game', I kept coming out of role to insist that they collaborate in creating an atmosphere of 'menace', appropriate to Pinter's text. Some students were, in fact, managing to 'threaten' me, but their efforts were often understated or even unnoticed by their peers because everyone was too *busy* following individual tacks.

I came out of role at first, trying to be positive: 'I was beginning to feel pressured . . . Do you realise what you were doing to make me feel uncomfortable . . .?', hoping, of course, that by making *everyone* conscious of what one or two were successfully doing they would all pick it up. I further referred to the script: 'Do you remember how Pinter uses a little bit of dialogue . . . and then a silence . . . and then . . . so it's not the *amount* of talking that is threatening . . . if you all wait for my answer to *one* question – that turns my stomach over . . .'.

As soon as the teacher intervenes in this way, clearly intellectualising the activity, s/he is inviting the class to switch to the demonstrating mode, working technically *within* the dramatic playing context. But then, as the students try out the teacher's ideas, it is possible that the momentum of the previous existential playing takes over once more. This began to happen on this occasion, but I was far from satisfied and interrupted twice more, as follows.

'Every time one person speaks, *use* it – by the way you sit, by the angle of your head, by your silent waiting for my character's response . . . if you break that silent waiting by continually jabbering its like throwing a lot of tennis balls into the air without a sense of purpose, and I am let off the hook of having to find an answer, so try not to fill the silence following one question with just another question.' Then I added, 'And don't fidget!' – this to a youth who in my previous work with the group on a different text had played the central role and had carried his responsibilities extremely well. Today he had little to offer and his fidgeting, breaking the stillness that the group was beginning to find, may have been his way of showing disapproval of this new work, or he may have been trying to regain attention. (Unfortunately he was not within the frame of the camera, so a viewer could not see what I was referring to). Whatever the reason for this kind of behaviour, I believe it is the teacher's responsibility to deal with it, but this can only happen in this open, abrupt way when the descriptive mode is being employed. Only when you require the class to work on technique, as I did here, are you justified in this kind of instructional control. I knew that if the boy did not keep still he would continue to undermine the efforts of the group.

They restarted, concentrating on trying out techniques for effective tension, but I interposed, 'I'm sorry . . . we're *nearly* doing it very well . . . Do you realise Robert, you are destroying it?'.

Robert, the fidgety one, mumbled, 'He's making me laugh'.

'Can we in the last few moments of the lesson manage to do it *very* well?', I said, and they did achieve a mood that gave some weight to each line of dialogue and each action. There was a nice moment, for example, when one girl held a key in the flat of her palm and then withheld it from me as my character tried to reach for it. Slowly, very slowly, the existential mode seeped back here and there, but now within a disciplined art form.

As a teacher I was very pleased with what I saw as dramatic achievement. It was something of a shock, therefore, some years later on a British Council course when I found myself, along with others, viewing the video recording of this lesson. I was still feeling pleased with what I saw as timely and appropriate teacher-intervention when a friend, also watching, began to chuckle 'sympathetically' at what he saw as a failing drama context where the teacher was clutching at straws in an unsuccessful attempt to retrieve something. 'I know what it's like', he offered magnanimously, 'to find yourself in this kind of corner.' I was too taken aback to respond, but one other observer suggested that he thought it was 'working'. 'Oh no!', my friend said, 'Those students are not experiencing menace.'

Here we have a fascinating process of evaluation, the outcome of which is that the teacher thought he was doing rather well and an equally experienced observer thought the teacher was doing rather badly! I think the answer lies in the different evaluative assumptions to be made about the two modes of acting behaviour. On the surface the dramatic activity, even after my interruption, continued (aided by the camera lens) to look like existential experiencing, for we were still 'making up a play', but, of course, that is not the case. Once the teacher imposes ideas for technique in this way there is inevitably a change of gear, and it becomes a matter of trying out the teacher's suggested techniques rather than of *being* in the experience. Thus my friend was *right* that they were not 'feeling' but, in my view, *wrong* to expect that they should be. This is a case of confusion of thinking about criteria to be applied in respect of the two contrasted modes. I shall obviously need to return to this question in Chapter 7.

3 Teacher as Fellow Artist – Working from 'Inside the Drama'

Usually called '**teacher-in-role**' (T in R), this is the most important strategy in the Drama teacher's repertoire. Even teachers of other subjects occasionally find it useful. Just as a specialist-subject teacher or a Primary School teacher may pick up a piece of chalk, show a picture or ask the class a question, so s/he may, whenever it seems suitable, endow an individual pupil (just sitting at a desk in the normal classroom arrangement) with a role by asking the following kind of question:

1 'I understand you were in Neville Chamberlain's party when he returned from Hitler waving his bit of paper ... What went on at that treaty-making? ... What did you see?'
2 'Dr Fleming, it is many years now since you discovered penicillin ... How did it happen? ... And did you appreciate just how beneficial it was going to be?'
3 To Joseph, Jacob's favourite son, 'Did you deserve to be thrown down that pit?'.
4 'Living as you do in East Berlin, what does the wall coming down mean to you?'
5 'As managing director of a chemical firm, do you not feel any guilt at all the chemical waste you have poured into the ocean over the years?'
6 'Looking back on your life, Pip, do you have any regrets?'
7 'As a leader of the team planning this new town, can you tell us why you have chosen that particular locality?'

Whether or not the specialist-subject teacher springs this kind of question as a surprise, or prepares the students by explaining that s/he is going to ask a question of someone as if that person were in a particular situation, will depend on the previous experience of the class. (It would be a foolish teacher who confronted pupils with this technique without any warning!) Having heard one pupil's answer s/he may turn to another 'Dr Fleming', 'Pip' 'East Berliner', etc. and s/he may get a discussion going on the validity of their answers, before returning to other strategies appropriate to teaching his/her subject.

This is probably the simplest form of T in R: it will only last a few moments; the role the teacher is playing is very close to a teacher's everyday role, that of questioner; and the pupil who is temporarily put on the spot finds him/herself confronted by the teacher but almost immediately helped by the teacher's role. For instance if the pupil is over-embarrassed or non-plussed, the teacher can quickly recognise this by giving more manageable follow-up questions. Suppose a girl faced with Question 5 looks blank. The teacher can ease the pupil into the novel situation by adding, for example, 'How long have you been managing director? . . . Do you know that your predecessor was also responsible for dumping waste?' or, letting that particular pupil off the hook altogether, 'I'm not surprised you're not prepared to answer such a delicate question . . . Would you mind if I interviewed your fellow directors?', or, turning to the rest of the class, out of role, 'Any managing director is likely to find this an impossible question to answer. Do you have any suggestions as to how such a person might cope with a confrontation of this kind?', etc., etc. The teacher continues to adjust to the response or lack of it from particular pupils and the class as a whole. Here, in this crude but effective example, you can begin to see some of the techniques of T in R.

This process of the teacher continually adjusting his/her role to the responses of the class, while having in his/her head a clear target (in this case to do with pollution risk and responsibility – both *factual* and *moral* implications) which s/he will steer the minds of the pupils towards, is a feature of the technique. Ideally, s/he would aim at getting several members of the class to speak 'as if' they owned those roles, but s/he may, with an inexperienced class, have to content him/herself with only a few questions and answers '*in role*', just sufficient to stimulate interest and discussion '*out of role*'.

The *main purpose* of T in R is to do with *ownership of knowledge*. Even in the unambitious, fairly pedestrian examples above, where the non-drama teacher is simply asking a few questions, it is clear that by placing the pupil 'in context' there is a greater chance that learning of a different quality will occur. An imperative tension is created in which the pupils find themselves engaged at a level that goes beyond 'This is interesting' to 'This *must* be dealt with'. All learning is a matter of 'ownership'. We have many ways of moving towards it: through listening, talking through it, reading about it, directly experiencing it, reflecting upon it, applying it and reapplying it. Being 'in role' combines a number of these without being identical to any of them: it is more than listening and talking because 'in context' carries the extra dimension of responsibility; it is a different kind of 'reading', the symbolic medium being a social interaction rather than print; it is less than direct experience, lacking the power of actuality, yet it can be more than direct experience because of 'metaxis' (seeing from two worlds at the same time) giving a reflective edge to the role-play which direct experience often lacks; it has a sense of applying knowledge, but lacks the consequences of real application. Because it *combines* these characteristics it moves the learner towards 'ownership' in a dynamic way, affecting the *quality* of the learning. It is not surprising that training schemes and educational projects from all walks of life – medical, business, industrial and caring professional – are now widely using T in R as a method, often very mechanically (rather like drawing a diagram) in a way unrelated to drama as an art form, but nevertheless with some enthusiasm as its potential is realised.

It will be apparent that a key feature of T in R is that it places the interaction in the *present*, a present characterised by imperative tension. There is a critical difference between a teacher asking a pupil, 'If you were the managing director of a chemical firm, would you feel guilty about chemical waste poured into the ocean?', and, as if 'in role', addressing the pupil, 'As managing director of a chemical firm, do you feel any guilt at all the chemical waste you have poured into the ocean?'. There is an implication in the latter form of question that the questioner and the one questioned are together framed face-to-face in an occurring social context in which answers are *demanded*. The responder is 'hooked' into the dramatic present. It is an invitation to participate in the existential present. The responder may be 'thrown' by this challenge, by not being sure of what the implicit 'rules of the game' are, but it is this very edge of uncertainty that contributes to the degree of alertness in the pupils, which in turn enhances the potential for learning.

T in R, as I have so far described it, appears to assume an unevenness in the distribution of power: the teacher has the idea; the teacher uses the technique to set up the dramatic playing interaction; the teacher begins to lose power as s/he adjusts to the answers; and the teacher decides when to terminate the exercise. As I analyse this method further you should remember that the exercise does not have to be teacher-initiated – a *pupil* can use the T in R technique with another pupil, or pupils with other pupils, or pupils with the teacher. Any occurrence in the drama where one person or group of persons attempts to bring the fictitious context firmly into the 'here and now' is using the T in R function. An obvious example of this technique used by pupils is in the occasion of 'hot-seating' when, immediately following the performance of a play, members of the audience put the actors on the spot by asking questions of the 'characters'. This is an example of the 'dramatic playing' activity initiated by the pupils.

So far I have based this discussion on a very limited form of T in R. We have assumed that the activity is not necessarily being seen as 'drama', but rather as History, or Religious Studies, or Literature, etc., and that its structure is strictly a 'question-and-answer' form. We need to move away from this crude version now towards seeing the teacher as fellow artist.

Teacher as fellow artist

First we have to give attention to what is the basic nature of drama for, until this is clear, what follows in the rest of this chapter and, indeed, in the rest of the book will not make sense.

I work on the assumption that drama is primarily about social events. Even where a play appears to be about a particular character, it is inevitably about that person in a series of social contexts. It is often the social contexts that mould the character. There are very few plays that appear to concentrate on a protagonist's inner or spiritual progress without reference to other people. The extreme examples that spring to mind are *Everyman* (anon.) and *Dr Faustus* (Marlowe), but the agonies of the central character in each of these plays are reflected through the other characters with which the two dramatists people the stage.

Thus I assume that drama par excellence is about social interaction, and this principle applies as much to play-making in the classroom as to stage plays. This assumption has a considerable effect on how one sets about creating drama in the classroom, for one's starting point is a social context and not, as some drama teachers have it, a characterisation. If you believe in the latter, then inevitably your introductory work with children in drama will concentrate on activities to do with 'building character': who *you* are; the kind of person you are; your background, your age, etc. I am not saying that this would never be my starting point, but rarely do I put a focus on an individual in this way. This view runs contrary to the philosophy and practice of pioneers in Child Drama, such as Brian Way (1967) and Margaret Faulkes. For them 'the individuality of the individual' is paramount. I would go so far as to say that their emphasis represents a misuse of the art form of drama which, as I said earlier, is essentially social. Nevertheless, there are times when such an approach seems eminently appropriate. For instance I recently participated in a workshop led by the Drama therapist,

Robert Landy, of New York University, in which we were asked to invent, individually, an identity for ourselves. This seemed appropriate in a therapy context, where the focus was on the individual's capacity for extending his repertoire of roles and for living a particular role more fully.

For the most part, however, I claim that our *initial* focus, or 'pre-text' as Cecily O'Neill (1982) calls it, must serve the art form of drama by creating a tacitly or explicitly agreed social context. To achieve this we draw on those resources that are available to us in everyday life, resources to do with signalling to each other what the context is, and to do with finding behaviour patterns that fit logically within that context. Just as in 'real life', however, individual members of a group may be idiosyncratically different from each other. The successful establishment of a social context is dependent on what they have in common. Thus they share a label of 'meeting attenders', or 'party-goers', or 'church congregation', or 'sport fans', and so on. As discussed in Chapter 1 (p. 3), participants at a party, however individually orientated, all have to 'work at' what they have in common – in this case being 'party-goers'.

Thus the starting point for 'dramatic playing' is nearly always to do with what the characters have in common. Let me hasten to say here that, once the social context is established, the emerging differences (what we call 'characterisation') may become very important to the drama experience. Notice that I use the word 'emerge', for by working this way we *discover* from the work as it proceeds what aspects of individuality seem most relevant. But here I am talking about the *early* stages of the work, and it is then that T in R plays a vital part. I shall now examine some of the ways in which this strategy operates.

Finding a focus

It is often the teacher's responsibility to adopt the function of a playwright and to find a focus. This focus should create the kind of imperative tension likely to appeal to that particular class of pupils and should provide a vehicle for the themes and images to be explored. Let me give some examples from my own practice:

1. In a dramatic playing about Robin Hood (the children's choice) with nine/ten-year olds, I placed the children 'in role' as craftsmen of a Nottinghamshire village. Under pressure from Robin Hood they were persuaded to switch temporarily to arrowmaking so that he and his men might storm the Sheriff's castle. I played the role of a messenger from

Robin Hood with this urgent request. Contrasting implementations of this lesson sequence are discussed in Chapter 5.

2 In setting up a drama with adolescents to parallel Miller's *The Crucible*, I used the role of meeting-house pastor to challenge the class (parents and children of the Puritan congregation) to find out which children had been 'dancing naked in Salem woods last night'.

3 In creating a drama about Halloween with six-year olds, as chief Witch I led the trainee witches into a 'humans'' school, right into a classroom 'where six-year old "humans" learn things'. 'Let's see what strange things *they* have to learn . . . Oh look! They've drawn portraits of us on their walls . . . What do you think they learn from these things?' (picking up a reading book, etc.). One of my purposes, of course, was to get the children to look at what education means.

Notice in each example how the group members are treated as if they are of the same kind – village craftsmen, Puritan families or trainee witches. It is as the drama proceeds that interesting differences emerge. In the first example individuals stood out, when it seemed appropriate, as: 'head of family; as a Robin Hood loyalist; as a pragmatist conscious of the 'long arm of the law'; as the one who knew most about making arrowheads; or as the one who was prepared to lie, for the sake of the rest of the village, to the sheriff's man. All these seeds of characterisation germinated from the drama and were therefore integral to it. These important differences can only be enjoyed when the social context is firmly established.

It is, however, the *choice of focus* that contributes to the work as art. Some uses of drama in schools, for instance **Simulation**, seek in a mechanical way to teach facts and practise associated skills, whereas the art form of drama *engages* with knowledge and opens up its implications. Shakespeare's *Troilus and Cressida* does not present facts about war but, rather, engages us, as Best (1985) suggests, in what those facts *amount to*. Also, Shakespeare funnels our entry into the military decisions through the lovesick eyes of Troilus. It is this kind of choice of focus that turns information about war on its head and allows us to see it anew. T.S. Eliot in (Part I of) *Murder in the Cathedral* takes us into the murder of Becket through the eyes of the poor of Canterbury: 'What danger can be, For us, the poor, the poor women of Canterbury?'.

Choice of the 'way in' to whatever the content is can be a determining factor in whether or not the classroom drama work moves into the art form, or stays as 'imitating the world out there'. Much inadequate drama, skill training and Simulation tend to rely on the latter. The importance of focus in relation to the art form is readdressed in Chapter 6.

Signalling the context

Objects, actions and words can help to 'build belief':

1. The teacher laying out a map, stabbing a particular spot with a knife, is quite a strong visual beginning for a 'Pirates hunting for treasure' drama with eight-year olds.
2. 'Swear on this bible', says the T in R to the Puritan daughters. (It is important that it is not actually a bible, of course.)
3. 'Let us put our witch's hats on . . .'. Nothing there of course, it is just a mimed sign, for if real hats were used (as inexperienced teachers might go for) their awkwardness to handle and perverseness in fitting correctly would signal the *opposite* of a witches' meeting; it would just show how fragile belief is when recalcitrant paper hats fall on the floor and get trampled on at the wrong moment!
4. 'Let's sit in a circle round this emblem of our tribe.'
5. The teacher silently reading a letter, then hurriedly folding it and putting it away deep in a pocket saying, 'You've not seen this . . . remember!', might provide a dramatic start to any drama where the plot has to be kept secret.

Please note that, in the process of 'building belief' in a drama, there is no particular virtue in 'keeping the drama going at all costs'. Part of the 'building belief' process may include stopping the drama every other minute to see whether the students can believe in what is being created. So, for instance, one drama I created with six-year olds started something like this: 'In a moment I am going to start a story, by doing something. I'm not going to tell you what it is . . . you'll have to guess . . . and I'll keep stopping to ask you what you've seen me do.'. I used T in R as a soldier marching up and down in front of the children who were sitting on the classroom floor. 'What have you seen . . . I wonder . . . Shall I carry on?' This time the 'soldier' sighed and yawned. 'What have you seen now? . . . Shall I . . . ?', and so on. This establishing the makebelieve both in *and* out of role is a useful double device for 'building belief'. Indeed, coming *out* of role is just as important in teaching drama as going into it!

Another example involves placing responsibility on the members of the class for building your role. Of course, their belief in the role becomes cemented because of their part in creating it. For instance with four-year olds the teacher says, 'What kind of witch do you want me to be?'

'A wicked one.'

'How wicked?'

'Very wicked'.

'What shall I have to do to be as wicked as that? ... Can you show me and I'll try to copy? ...'

Similarly with a class of eighteen-year olds on the theme of AIDS: 'Okay, I'll be the AIDS patient in this hospice ... Do you want me to be male or female? ... Do you want me to be heterosexual or homosexual? ... Do you want me to be married or single?...'. It is worth noting that, even when the 'character' was built according to the class's satisfaction and the drama, which in this case started with the group as journalists interviewing the patient, I continued to place responsibility on the class by breaking off from my role intermittently, inviting them to comment on and, if necessary, adjust how I was playing the part.

Think back for a moment to one of the theoretical aspects I discussed in Chapter 2 (p. 16). It was argued that in dramatic playing activity there tend to be at least two phases of acting behaviour. Initially, a great deal of signalling may be going on where the participants are 'working at' establishing the fictitious context. Such signalling is characterised by its *descriptive quality*. However, once the fiction is under way the participants' acting behaviour imperceptibly takes on an existential quality of submitting to and trusting the social event. So, for instance, if a group were making a drama about a scene in a Salem meeting-house, its members' acting behaviour would be likely to change from descriptive to existential. When the leader of the group (usually a teacher, of course) uses T in R, then s/he tends to take upon him/herself the signalling responsibility, so that *the leader's acting behaviour is purely descriptive – and remains so*. I cannot think of any occasion I have observed or participated in where the teacher has submitted to the existential experience. This would seem to be inappropriate teacher-behaviour. On the other hand, given that the leader is carrying the burden of *establishing the fiction*, the participants, freed from that particular burden, can submit to the existential experience. Thus the technique of T in R advances the quality of the students' engagement towards the spontaneity of the dramatic present. In the above example of the Salem meeting-house, if the teacher takes on the role of the Reverend Minister then his/her behaviour is purely descriptive, while inviting the participants to submit to the moment-to-moment experiencing of the fictitious social event. Pictorially, the use of T in R could be shown as in the next figure.

Introducing a formal or aesthetic dimension

Here again it is probably useful to give an example from practice. I was visiting an Infant School to watch a mature teacher who had just joined my

Teacher-in-role

Teacher
'signalling'
'describing',
'demonstrating'

part-time drama course. This required me to observe and help members of the course in the classroom. On this particular occasion she had been doing drama related to the story of Moses bringing the Israelites out of Egypt. The class had reached the point of being stranded in a desert area and needing to explore different parts of the terrain with a view to finding the 'promised land'. So off they went in small groups to different parts of the hall, following instructions that they were to be prepared to 'report back' on whatever they found. After about five minutes they clustered round their teacher full of chatter, competing with each other in terms of what they had seen by way of rivers, hills, rich soil, wildlife, domestic animals, vegetation or the lack of them, etc. Not surprisingly the teacher, bombarded in this way, found herself pleading, 'One at a time so that I can hear.'. Then she had a bright idea: she quietened everybody and announced that, as 'Moses' was sitting over there (pointing in my direction!), they should move over and report to me, which they did in a rush!

Pause to analyse what is going on and you discover a kind of 'playing' that fails to be dramatic. Certainly the children are adopting an existential, 'here and now' mode, but it should not be mistaken for drama for there is little that gives the participants (either consciously or unconsciously) a sense of form. *My* responsibility was to try to use the same material to create the excitement of theatre. What I did was very simple, but it had the effect of making every action and every word seem important, and this is what art is.

I began by using the T in R method suggested above (p. 37), getting the class to tell me how to play Moses, but my questions started to look at Moses in terms of *space*: 'How big a tent would Moses have? . . . Can we pace it out? . . . Where will the entrance be? . . . How will you know that it is your *leader's* tent? ... Will there be guards? ... Where? ... If the entrance is there, where will Moses sit? ...'.

I asked the whole class, except for the two newly chosen guards who were now standing either side of the 'entrance', to stand against the far wall. They watched as I engaged in the following kind of dialogue with one of my 'guards':

MOSES: Have my people returned from their search for the promised lands?

GUARD: Yes.

MOSES: They will be weary, but time is short; it is necessary that we hear their reports on what they have found. It is very hot in this desert and I am old. Before they come in, please bring a bowl of water.

(The 'water' was brought in.)

Dip your fingers into the water and place its coolness on my parched lips.

(He did this.)

Thank you. Now I am ready to see my people. Is the first group there?

GUARD: Yes.

MOSES: Tell them that they might approach the entrance of my tent. Do not forget to ask them their business before you allow them to enter.

(The group approached and, pikes at the ready, the entrance was barred until they had explained why they had come.)

MOSES (as the group entered): As the first to return, please take your proper place.

(I indicated an area near my chair.)

(And so each group went through this ritual. Note that the tent area we had established was big enough to hold the whole class of 30 – very important.)

MOSES (formally, as I turned to the first group): Do you have a spokesperson? Please proceed.

(Each was heard in turn.)

MOSES: It must be your decision. Will you please indicate which of the lands reported on seems most favourable.

(A vote was taken.)

MOSES: Very well; I wish you God's speed. As your leader I have finished what I had to do. I will not be with you much longer, children of Israel. Go to the promised land.

Using theatre in this brief episode I attempted to establish imagery of old age, hierarchy of leadership, desert, significance of the 'chosen land' and an almost ritualistic procedure for making a choice. It was mostly achieved through the formality of language *and* the formality of space.

Similarly in the Salem drama, the 'meeting-house' scene demanded that each family knew where each member sat (head of the family on the aisle) and then: 'Will you ask your eldest daughter to stand . . . Come here child . . . You know this book is the word of God? . . . Place your hand on it . . . firmly child . . . Now say after me . . . my soul is innocent . . . look me in the eye child', and so on.

Notice that, in both these examples, the teacher is playing an authoritative role. This is often the case when, in the early stages of the drama, you want the class to have a dramatic experience. But it is not the only kind of role available to the teacher, as the following examples show.

1 As part of a story about an 'alien' landing on Earth by mistake, with the class (remedial) as 'earthlings' and me as the frightened alien, I am crouched at the furthest point away from them and, as they approach, try to retreat behind furniture. Again, space is significant.

2 In a French Revolution context, the class set up a 'people's court', formally arranging themselves in a three-quarters circle. I, with a few others, have to enter the circle in order to plead for the release of a prisoner.

Teacher as narrator

Although it may not seem so when it is actually happening, when a drama is over it becomes a story – you can often hear children abstracting the 'plot' from the drama experience they have just had and repeating it to other people. This occurs all the time in everyday life. When something is happening to us we do not think of it as a story, but if it has been interesting we cannot wait to find an audience in order to turn it into one.

In working in drama as an art form it is occasionally possible for *the teacher* to harness the narrative form in the service of the dramatic experience. (I showed in the Chapter 2 (p. 18) how the *pupils* can become narrators.) In some circumstances the teacher or a pupil can narrate as action is taking place, for instance in creating a particular mood or atmosphere. This is especially useful in a situation where small groups are scattered over a classroom or hall space and, because of their 'busy' dramatic playing, need to be drawn gently into the same play: 'As the noon heat settled over their village, no energy was wasted on words; silently they bent to pick the fruit, each full basket being carried to the loading area; time seemed to stand still; all occupied in the same task; no one knew what was in their private thoughts . . .'.

The last line, of course, is the storyteller's ploy of building tension through anticipation. Having 'planted' this, the teacher, if it fits in with the class's plans, could then introduce the new shift in the drama by continuing: 'They certainly did not know what *one* of their people was thinking . . . they did not notice that Sara had stopped filling her basket . . .', and so on.

Think back to the 'sanctuary' drama described in Chapter 2 (p. 21). On that occasion the monks were at prayer when the child, in role as a stranger, hammered at the sanctuary door. If you were working with an inexperienced class, or felt for some reason that the particular child needed to be 'cued in', you could use narration: 'As the monks knelt at their prayer desks absorbed in their late evening service of compline, their pious silence was suddenly shattered . . . (the child knocks) . . . They continued to pray, disciplined by their order of worship . . . but then the knock was heard again . . . (clearly an instruction to the 'stranger') . . . This time a monk arose, left the chapel and unbolted the heavy door . . . (again, using narration to instruct)'. Notice that the kind of behaviour resulting from such instruction is nearer to 'illustrative/performance', for the volunteer 'monk' is not *living* the situation; he is merely demonstrating carrying out the narrator's instructions. *But* from this moment narration ceases and the exercise moves into spontaneous 'dramatic playing'.

Teacher as teacher!

Working 'from the inside', a teacher can use his/her role to *control* irrelevant behaviour, that is:

- from a particular individual, well-intentioned but illogical behaviour that is in danger of 'throwing' the rest. (Notice that if it does not upset the rest, you will often let it pass for the time being, intending to refer to it later if necessary), or
- deliberately destructive behaviour, from someone who wants to have that kind of power or who is losing interest or is bored. (Don't forget that, because we are working in the art form, there must be times when the work sags with boredom and frustration. All artists understand this very well!)

In the Pinter example (Chapter 2, p. 29) you saw how the teacher can come out of role in order to manage behaviour: 'Don't fidget!', I insisted. But sometimes a teacher will use his role to isolate the recalcitrant character (notice the 'character', not the child), reprimand him/her, argue with him/her, challenge him/her, deflect him/her, offer an alternative route for him/her or even elevate the character. Any one of these may be appropriate according to how the teacher 'reads' what is going on. The important thing is that the teacher can bring about a change in destructive behaviour *from 'the inside'* of the creativity.

Sometimes, of course, the teacher needs to *promote* particular behaviour. For instance s/he can use his/her influence from 'within' the drama to 'create space' for the shy child, or the child whose significant offering was ignored or just not heard by the rest of the group. All it needs is something like, 'This witch thinks we should leave before dawn', or simply, 'I think Mary's idea seems a good one'. Sometimes it is *literally* space that is needed: 'Let us all move back so that the president can address us . . .'.

Symbolisation

The word 'symbol' is often best avoided as it has so many different meanings for people. Its most common usage among drama practitioners is in saying that drama is a symbolic medium. The danger of this is that it gives the impression that when something is expressed in drama it 'stands for' something else – back to a mimetic concept. My preference is to use/ **symbolisation**, suggesting a *process*. The process is experienced either by an audience in a theatre or during dramatic playing, especially when the dramatic playing is sustained over a period of time. *Time* is an important factor, for symbolisation is to do with gradual accretion of meaning. At first an object, action or sound is simply read as a 'sign', or is not even read at all. Only gradually does it gather significance in our minds, like the recurring image of the handkerchief, 'spotted with strawberries', that in Shakespeare's *Othello* becomes the pivot of Othello's disintegration.

In George Tabori's *Mein Kampf: Farce*, the simple act of the Jew offering the young Adolf his coat passes barely unnoticed until, as the play proceeds, that simple act of charity begins to symbolise the act of submission by the Jews. General Gabler's pistols become a symbol of the dead father's power over his daughter Hedda in Ibsen's *Hedda Gabler*. In Pinter's *The Caretaker* the bag that begins as a sign of Davies' luggage becomes, as the play continues, a symbol of both his past history and of his intrusion into the brothers' lives.

In the 'dramatic playing' activity one can observe the power of the symbolisation process. What begins as a sign grows in significance. So, for example, in working with adolescents on the theme of a mother leaving her family behind, her shopping bag became an important element in the exercise. In early episodes it simply signalled 'mother', towards the end of the drama experience, after she had left home leaving her bag behind her, it symbolised the severance from her family and her past role as domestic drudge in that family.

It is unlikely that this kind of accumulated meaning can occur in the illustrative/performance mode, as such 'instant coffee' tends not to be sustained long enough for such change.

My favourite example of this symbolisation process in action dates from many years ago. I was teaching a large class of ten/eleven-year olds about how the 'Dust Bowl' of central America forced the farmers to journey over the Rockies to the 'promised land' of California. In their drama the children experienced, in families, packing up to leave home (Oklahoma), being cheated by truck-hire firms and crossing the Rockies. Then, inviting them just to sit side-by-side in their trucks with their eyes closed, I narrated the dawn: 'They had struggled through many trials. The physical hardships had been such that many thought they would never make it, but this morning their trucks were parked on gentler slopes and in the near distance the early sun shone on the green lushness of California . . .'. Then, as teacher, 'Now open your eyes and make your descent . . .'. What they met was a Californian (T in R), standing on a high rock (chair) to peer at them as they slowly made their approach (across the space of the school hall). He had an orange in his hand (a sign of California).

As they came near it occurred to me that I could *extend* the use of the orange. This recognition of the potential metaphor within the act of handling an orange is the kind of intuitive, spontaneous act that can occur when one is working 'inside' the action. As I addressed the crowd, 'What you folks doing trespassing? . . .', I started to eat the orange, dropping the peel at their feet: an insult and an injustice. The children's immediate reaction was the one to be expected from ten-year olds – they shouted abuse at the Californian, demanding to be let in and claiming their rights. We broke off the drama, giving them time to reflect on the stalemate situation. They planned a new approach, an apologetic one. In fact they verbally grovelled to the Californian farmer, who listened to them (as he ate his second orange – now a 'symbol' of an unfair power situation) and then said, 'I'm glad you 'Okies' have had the decency to apologise. Now go back to where you came from.'!

At this point (when, no doubt, I could have been lynched!) their History teacher, my friend John Fines who had been the one who suggested the orange to me in the first place, stepped in and explained, 'That is how it was'. He then filled them in with further historical detail, explaining to them that the destitute travellers had either to return home or face being put in camps as 'displaced persons'.

About a year later there was an interesting sequel to this lesson. I was in California running a course for teachers. At one point I described the 'Dust Bowl' lesson to them. An uncomfortable silence was broken by a deeply offended member of my class asking why I would choose to put America in such a terrible light by distorting history in this way. 'No way could it be true; Californians are just not like that!'. Fortunately for me (I was probably in danger of getting lynched again!), another voice from the group said, 'Oh but they are the facts – my grandparents were put in those camps.'! Some examples of symbolisation from more recent teaching are described below.

When I set up the 'Sanctuary' drama (pp. 21 & 42) we started by placing two chairs as a 'sign' of where the sanctuary door was. Interestingly, I have done this drama twice to date, once with a Grade 4 class in New York, then just three months later with a group of teachers in Vancouver. In the case of the work with the pupils, the drama eventually centred on the discovery that the sanctuary-seeker had the plague. The two chairs 'signing' the entrance became unimportant and were virtually forgotten. With the adult class, however, the interest started to centre on whether the stranger would have the courage to leave sanctuary voluntarily to face the justice of the land that awaited him, by the door he had first entered. In this scenario as those 'in role' all face the door, giving him the choice of going through it or returning to his cell, the door can become part of the metaphor for the stranger's decision.

Notice this '*can* become'. We cannot assume that the students in our classes are sensitive to such symbolism. The teacher must be wary of picking up resonances where none exist for the participants. There is a danger that, because the teacher sees those two chairs as a significant symbol of the stranger's refuge, s/he keeps pushing for the class to make that same recognition when in fact some members of the class may still be having difficulty even acknowledging that there is a door there! – they haven't even 'owned' the 'sign'. I will return to this subject later when achievement in drama is discussed in Chapter 7 (p. 135).

A few weeks ago, in working on the theme of child sexual abuse with a group of adults who had suffered as children, we invented a child, Kate. At first we simply used an empty chair with a doll on it to represent Kate – a sign that she was there, something to be referred to and talked *about*. As we proceeded to build up Kate's relationship with her father it was interesting to notice how the empty chair could be talked *to*, and even hugged and caressed.

In a drama related to the 'Pied Piper' story, the 'townsfolk' were at one point invited each to take a fairly large piece of paper and draw their fears of what might happen if the plague of rats got worse. When it did spread and their pleas continued to be ignored by the Town Councillors, they proceeded ritualistically to tear up their drawing papers under the Councillors' very noses. This is an interesting use of another art form which in itself becomes a symbolic means of expression within the drama.

In a drama about football supporters the scarves that initially acted as signs of 'who we are' took on other meanings when one character used his for hanging himself.

The sweat band that initiated us into a desert tribe became a symbol of respect when one of our number failed to return.

Perhaps the most poignant example of symbolisation I can recall is when Dorothy Heathcote was working with a group of institutionalised adolescent boys on the theme of 'Death of Kennedy'. As part of the fiction, set in a prison on the morning one of the inmates (Kennedy's killer) was to go to the electric chair, she had one of the 'characters' wash part of the 'prison' floor with a mop and bucket. There seems nothing remarkable about this 'sign', until you recall who the participants were – this was an institution for young offenders. Thus in the drama Dorothy was creating a prison for young people who were already prisoners. As this final phase of their drama began, each 'prison inmate' was lying with closed eyes on his bed listening to the early morning sounds. For these particular boys the swish of a mop on the floor symbolised captivity and servility more effectively than anything else. (Washing floors was a daily routine.) The sound of that single action created the fictitious prison and allowed their thoughts to centre on 'the condemned man'.

Having mentioned Dorothy Heathcote, this is a good point to give some attention to her method of working as fellow artist within the drama.

'Mantle of the expert' approach

This is a phrase Dorothy Heathcote (see Johnson & O'Neill, 1984) coined to describe a particular method of teaching that has characterised her approach to drama and education during the last twenty years. The '**Mantle of the expert**' (M of E) technique is a method that in latter years she has employed for some 90 per cent of her work with Primary School children, especially when there has been a need to cover the full curriculum. As you will discover, it offers a rich dramatic seam. Unfortunately it has not always been sufficiently well understood, and people like me have been guilty of teaching a watered-down version with inadequate results. In

Chapter 5, where I give examples of classroom practice, I have played safe by using examples of M of E from Dorothy's past repertoire (pp. 99 & 105) rather than risking describing my own. I hope she will feel I do the method justice in my attempt to explain it here!

I have included the M of E approach in this chapter on 'Teacher-in-role' because it is a method that, in its early stages and for the greater part of the work, is dependent on teacher and class belonging to the same fictitious organisation. Also, it is invariably the teacher's choice of context that is critical to the learning that goes on, although the *topic* may be the class's choice. Here is a simple example. A class of eight/nine-year olds wanted to do a drama about 'robots'. A typical 'drama' way of starting (which is from my own teaching) might involve scientists meeting secretly to build a robot that is going to outstrip all other robots – the robot is going to be able to think for itself! This is a useful way of getting young children to consider concepts such as 'thinking' and 'autonomy'. I began the drama by asking the 'scientists' (I was 'in role' as a 'go-between', acting for them and a wealthy entrepreneur) what kind of knowledge the robots would need in order to start thinking. They decided that adding and subtracting numbers was essential. I cast myself temporarily as a robot. (That is I 'stood in' for a robot while not attempting to *be* the robot but rather representing an idea to be tested. This is a good example of the deployment of the descriptive mode within dramatic playing. There is a subtle double role here of both representing the go-between and having the go-between temporarily 'stand in' for the robot in order to try something out. This allows the go-between role to say things like, 'Am I getting this 'robot' voice right?'.) I waited to be taught. We had immediate problems which we came out of role to discuss. When I went back into 'standing in' we had a better idea of how to set about handling a robot and 'feeding' it with arithmetical concepts; part of the work involved going into pairs, with one partner as a 'scientist' and the other as a 'stand-in robot'.

On the surface this appears to be a M of E approach in that the pupils are in role as 'experts' and there is a problem of a practical kind to be solved. However, Dorothy would argue that in such a short time one cannot expect the children to become experts simply by endowing them with that role, although the endowment has to begin the process. What they bring to the problem may not be much more than whatever resources *they already have* as individual members of the class. Because of the way drama operates *some* learning will have taken place, for instance the very focusing of the drama will have sharpened up the problem and their understanding of it. There is also a good chance that the fiction will have given a collective impetus to the activity, perhaps motivating the children beyond their individual imaginative selves. Through its focus it may also have cast a new light on the potential power of robots and what is meant by 'thinking' and 'autonomy'. However, because this whole process was rushed into two or three drama lessons, it relied too much on the children merely wearing the label of 'expert' rather than *earning* it. Therefore the many levels of achievement, in terms of skills and knowledge, were likely to fall a long way short of what eight/nine-year olds are capable of over a longer period of time using M of E as the sophisticated form it really is.

The true M of E approach requires a long-term project lasting several days or spread over several weeks. Suppose that, instead of using the kind of dramatic method outlined in my lesson above, I intended to switch to a M of E approach using the same themes. The teaching of knowledge to the robots could conceivably still be a central experience for the pupils. That does not have to change, *but* the experience would occur much later in the work *when their sense of collective expertise and a recognition of the considerable responsibility that goes with such expertise* were well-established. This happens when the pupils see themselves as experts rather than 'pretending to be' experts. It should be noted that taking on a role of 'expert' appears, at first sight anyway, to be of a different order from taking on the role of 'a witch', a 'treasure-hunter', a 'monk' or an 'engine-driver'. While one can 'get by' with adopting such labels in order to create a drama, because 'expert' is an *attitude* and not merely a title the role demands that the role-player actually *has* that attitude. It is inadequate to 'demonstrate' being an expert through descriptive signalling alone (although in the *early* stages of M of E, as in all dramatic playing, this is likely to be all that happens). Of course, ultimately, some of the differences are eclipsed, for if children are to sustain the role of 'witch', 'treasure-hunter', 'monk' or 'engine-driver', developing such roles will entail the group's identifying and absorbing the attitudes that such characters have towards what they do. But the key difference lies in the intended 'obsessiveness' (using the term in its most positive sense) about their work and sense of responsibility towards it that become a necessary part of the make-up of the 'experts'. The concept of 'imperative tension,' that there are tasks that *must* be done, is supremely exemplified in the M of E approach.

Thus in the M of E version of my 'robot' project, by the time the central activity of 'teaching the robot' is reached the pupils should be well-established as a group of experts – over many hours of preceding work they have come to recognise that they have *earned* that title. The quality of their knowledge about robots and the capacity they have had for hard thinking and studying on the subject has gradually been enhanced by a series of carefully graded experiences within the fictitious context of, say, 'Running a robot laboratory'. By the time they reach the central point of *my* lesson there is a very good chance they will be much better informed about programming. *They* may suggest that someone should 'stand in' for a while as a robot (for such a demonstrating method will be part of their resources). Above all, to the teacher's question, 'What kind of knowledge should we start with?', there are going to be *more* answers, and more *carefully considered* answers, especially in the light of implications of the proposed actions. Some bright children may foresee trouble in the notion of having thinking, autonomous robots, and may express doubts about taking on the contract on ethical grounds!

'Contract' is an operative word. Invariably Dorothy will set up an agency. From the beginning she has a choice of context, a choice of what kind of agency it should be. If she already knows that she is steering towards getting the children to look at the nature of learning and knowledge, then the 'robot laboratory' context seems logical. On the other hand, the work can spring from a context of a more general kind, and the 'robot project' just happens to come along as one of many other disparate contracts. In Chapter 5 I describe in detail a M of E lesson which starts as a 'Lettuce warehouse' and where the employees eventually finish up 'making heroes'!

Let us assume that our hypothetical M of E exercise is going to start with the pupils as 'robot makers'. In the following paragraph I outline some suggestions as to how Dorothy might begin the work.

Dorothy's first instinct is to establish a past history for the agency, so she will set around the classroom different kinds of sign (robot diagrams; laboratory rules; letters of thanks from past clients referring to 'past' successful contracts pinned to a 'staff' noticeboard; an incomplete staff holiday roster, etc.) and the language she employs in starting the drama will be of an oblique kind that presupposes a long-standing relationship as professionals. She will have a few questions, the kind where children can grab answers 'out of the air': 'Have any of you been working on that toy contract? . . . I know some of you were worried about size for four-year olds to handle . . . Did you decide on a size that's manageable? . . . Yes, he won't always have his mother around . . . Perhaps we should give more thought to safety . . . There's a contract here for electronic doors . . . Can anyone remember? . . . Have we done doors before? . . . Sorry about the power cut last week . . . We are going to have the whole laboratory rewired . . .', and so on.

Then she might move forward to a simple task, which may or may not grow out of some of their answers. Although she is preparing them to move into small groups round tables, each group starting on some 'new contract in this morning's mail', a necessary step before they have small-group responsibility may be to have them all do the same task, one which guarantees quick and successful results: 'We seem to have a lot of new contracts in today's mail ... I've sorted out which I think should have priority ... (She knows that in later work *they* might well decide on priorities) ... But before you start on those, could I trouble you to give me your early reactions to the new lighting system we'll be installing? ... The electricians say we could have different kinds of lamps if we like ... we don't have to keep them all the same ... I wonder if you could do a quick drawing of the kind of lamp you would like over *your* desk ... just to give us all an idea of what our favourite styles of lampshades and things are ... Have a good look at the laboratory ceiling ... Yes, I know its dirty at present, but we'll have that painted up before your new lights are fixed ... See if you can picture what kind of lamp you want over your work ... Perhaps you and your colleague will consider and then let the secretary know ...'.

Thus the experience proceeds in a modest way, with a task that will be easily accomplished and which also begins to establish a sense of place, a 'laboratory environment', and a sense of the students having control over it. From this the small groups can be initiated into practical 'robot' tasks. Then when belief in their status in *that* laboratory is established: 'Someone here ... it's today's mail ... wants us to teach robots to think for themselves ... Whatever next?! ... I'll pin the letter on the noticeboard ... If you've got time to have a look at it ... you can tell me what I should reply ...'. So, those aspects of the work that are critical, as far as the teacher is concerned, are 'dropped in' quite casually when the time is ripe.

Of course, the casual approach is deceptive. The teacher uses a restricted language code deliberately and with care. When they do move into small-group tasks the teacher's function is that of 'empowerer' – encouraging, elaborating, elevating what individuals do and drawing the attention of the whole class to what any small group may be doing. In this way, although working separately, they all feel part of the same enterprise. Also, and most important, the teacher will be 'dropping in' whatever accurate knowledge s/he feels the class is ready to hear.

The M of E approach promotes a kind of 'collective characterisation'. This has kinship with the rehearsal process actors go through in creating a character for a Theatre Performance, in that over a period of time the pupils develop their expertise and *become* experts, just as actors gradually *become* characters. Here the comparison stops, of course, for the critical differences remain: there is no written script, no repetition and little individualisation between one participant and another. M of E demands of the participants that together they develop a special way of seeing the world; they develop an attitude of respect and responsibility towards what they are doing to an extent that it becomes part of their value system; and, above all, the 'spectator' in them rigorously monitors everything they do and sets their actions against that value system.

In theoretical terms M of E is a perfect example of the use of the existential mode. Once the 'agency' (or whatever) is established, the participants are continually in the 'here and now' of the dramatic present. They are impelled by the 'imperative tension' created by the task. They carry out their recordings, their drawings, their planning meetings and their informal discussions with virtually no suggestion of descriptive acting behaviour, unless, as we have already seen in the 'robot stand-ins' (and as we shall see later in other examples), they *choose* to use such descriptive behaviour as one of their resources. When this happens it becomes an example, as explained in Chapter 2 (p. 28), of the use of well-defined illustrative/performance behaviour *within* the dramatic playing activity: the descriptive and the existential occur simultaneously within the fictitious frame.

4 Teacher as Fellow Artist – Working from 'Outside the Drama'

In the previous chapters I distinguished between descriptive and existential characteristics of acting behaviour. Of course, these two categories are theoretical props. In practice, as you have seen, there are times when it is difficult to distinguish which mode a particular pupil is adopting. Nevertheless, it is useful to retain them as separate concepts, for there are times when the difference is both clear and significant. This is true particularly in respect of dramatic exercises where pupils in small groups, or in pairs, work simultaneously and where the teacher remains firmly outside the experience.

Both teacher and pupil have to be clear as to the *purpose* of such an exercise. If it is set as, 'In your pairs, prepare a scene for us to see later in which a parent receives a son or daughter who has arrived home much later than promised', then clearly the teacher is indicating that they should harness their 'instant coffee' skills and work for credibility, repeatability and communicability. In the time they have to prepare it, clarity in all three dimensions will be uppermost in the pupils' minds – a perfectly legitimate exercise. If, however, it is set as, 'In your pairs, set up a situation in which a parent receives a son or daughter who has arrived home much later than promised. See what happens and we'll ask you to tell us about it afterwards', this implies that it is 'what happens' that matters. It is to be an experience to be reflected on and reported on, not to be repeated. The choice of acting mode is clear. Interestingly, in both cases there is an *end product*. In drama there is always a 'drama made', but it is the participants' knowledge of how the end product is to be used that actually affects how they set about creating it, for the process is critical, both in educational and artistic terms. The existential mode is invited by the second version, so consequently the quality of the experience is significantly different – not necessarily *better*, just *different*. Whether or not it is a better experience depends on what the class or the topic most needs at that time. It is unlikely that young children can benefit from either form: the descriptive mode places too early an emphasis on 'How do I look from the outside?'; sustaining the existential mode *as a pair's task set by the teacher* is often too difficult for young children – it is one thing for the teacher to appear to be playing *with* them by using T in R, but another matter to have the teacher *instruct* them in a dramatic playing *exercise*.

If, of course, you have a class of pupils whose sole diet of drama has been a variety of illustrative/performance activities, then no amount of rephrasing the instruction will guide them towards true dramatic playing. Indeed, they may feel there is no point in doing the exercise unless they are to show it to others. The reason for this, in part, is that for pupils of such limited experience there is little attraction in work of this kind unless there is the extra challenge of 'showing'. It seems to be a 'chicken-and-egg' situation *unless* the class is made aware that what it is creating in the dramatic playing activity demands a subtle handling of theatrical elements. Obviously, if they have had continual experience of drama they will be familiar with bringing formal elements to both the existential and descriptive modes. They will be conscious of the manipulation of space and time, and the use of elements such as surprise and contrast, but there is an aspect of 'dramatic tension' that they may not be so familiar with. It may initially be the responsibility of the teacher to inject this element into the dramatic playing exercise, so that the pupils feel they are indeed working in theatre as they experience, say, their parent/offspring interaction.

I should like to suggest that the above instruction to go into the parent/offspring pairs is inadequate if the class is to feel it is working in the *art* of drama. The exercise needs to include some aspect of *constraint*, a form of tension which I shall now examine in some detail.

Constraint

When I first studied drama seriously, one of the 'laws' that was drilled into me was that 'drama is *conflict*'. In subsequently running workshops in drama I faithfully followed this ideal by setting mother against son, brother against sister, town against town, state against state, and tribe against tribe. My workshops were characterised by the volume of vociferous hostility permeating the theatre studio, school hall or classroom. It was only on an occasion when we slipped into an improvisation where two parents were anxiously waiting for bad news, that it dawned on me that we had something intensely dramatic on our hands that had little to do with conflict.

Since then, through a study of play-texts, I have realised that what playwrights are really concerned with are *constraints*. Obviously, conflict is a necessary part of drama, but the expression of conflict is no more important, and indeed may be less important, than the *withholding* of it. If two people want to express their hostility or love towards each other, but for some reason are not free to do so, that can be more dramatic than their giving full vent to their feelings: in Shakespeare's *Twelfth Night*, Viola cannot declare her love for Orsino – when she does the play is over; in Shakespeare's *King Lear*, Goneril and Regan cannot explicitly declare to their father, 'We want to be rid of you' – they disguise their true feelings by appearing to be concerned about the size of his entourage. In most texts one or more characters are constrained in the expression of *true* feeling. On those rare occasions when there is virtually no constraint, either the whole play or that part of the play is over, or you can be sure that the audience knows or guesses that such an honest interaction cannot last, or that is is falling short in some way of being a true expression. Even the continual raging of the husband and wife in Albee's *Who's afraid of Virginia Wolf?* turns out to be a shared expression of pain at the couple's childlessness.

More common even than constraint on self-expression is the constraint on *true facts* being exposed. This provides the dynamic from a typical 'Whodunnit?' to *Oedipus Rex* where the whole play is given to a gradual unfolding of the truth. Another common form of constraint is the setting up of obstacles so that a character cannot do what s/he wants to do. In vain, Macbeth seeks supreme power. These two constraints, the withholding of facts and the inhibition on a character's wants, provide the substance for a play's plot. It is, however, the first kind of constraint mentioned above, the constraint on expression of feeling, that is of particular interest to workshop leaders and participants, for this kind of constraint affects the dynamic of every momentary interaction and so is relevant to even the briefest improvisation exercise.

We can attempt a categorisation of the constraints on true expression of feeling. They appear to be:

- physical;
- psychological;
- social;
- cultural;
- procedural;
- formal or technical.

These are not discrete divisions: it is not always possible to distinguish between what is psychologically and socially determined, or between what is socially and culturally determined. Nevertheless, it is useful for a teacher to separate them for they can provide the basis for selecting a workshop exercise. I shall now look at the typical 'pairs' exercise described at the beginning of this chapter (p. 52), to be carried out by a class of adolescents, using the well-tried theme of 'angry parent greets offspring who had promised to be home an hour ago'. It will be obvious that the choice of constraint brings a distinctly different texture to the experience.

Physical constraint

The parent has to vent his/her anger through the shut and locked door of the bedroom to which the offspring has rushed on arrival.

Psychological constraint

The parent is determined, for the sake of their future relationship, to control his/her angry feelings.

Social constraint

The parent is embarrassed because of the presence of a visiting relative, who has nobly offered to 'wait up' with the parent.

Cultural constraint

Because it is past midnight it is now the day of the parent's birthday, and the adolescent has brought home a birthday present!

Procedural constraint

The late daughter happens to be the Queen of England!

Formal or technical constraint

The offspring is totally deaf and relies on sign language, or the scene is to take place using animal characters as a metaphor – between 'parent rabbit' and 'adolescent bunny'!

Constraints have a pedagogical as well as dramatic implications. The drama lies in the constraint (often, you will notice, having a moral implication) on the character, but the participant, or actor, can also 'enjoy' the meaningful tension between the spoken and the unspoken. Paradoxically, it is the unspoken that is brought to mind *because expression of it is not allowed.* The teacher in the classroom can harness this paradox, for it means that the adolescent or adult participants can engage with themes like 'facing death', 'grief' or 'love' at a sub-focal or tacit level, while their focus of attention is on *not* expressing grief or love, etc. This means that 'heavy' material for improvisation that would normally be avoided, because the participants would tend to trivialise it rather than explicitly deal with it, can be tackled with the knowledge that it is to remain implicit. In this way, far from the theme becoming trivialised, it can be engaged with in safety at whatever level each participant is ready to cope with.

Imagine, for example, that the students are going to play the characters of the parents, grieving over the loss of their daughter. By insisting on some relevant constraint, such as 'refusing to talk to each other', 'silently blaming each other' or 'having to stay bright for the sake of the other daughter', there is a greater chance that not only will the scene be dramatic, but it will also be *significant* to the participants. They may get much nearer to a sense of grieving because they are not required to express it.

Breaking the constraint: temporary chaos!

If constraints are in themselves dramatic, then it is certainly true that 'breaking' them is equally dramatic. In Shakespeare's *The Winter's Tale*, Leontes eventually cracks and banishes Hermione from the court; Late in Miller's *Death of a Salesman*, Willie Loman painfully hears the truth from his son; in Shakespeare's *KingLear*, Lear is banished into the storm; Shakespeare's Hamlet turns on Ophelia; Shaw's *Pygmalion* is about that most common social constraint: social status, and Eliza Doolittle eventually has the guts to break it. To persist with a constraint too long is to lose the dynamic of the drama. For this reason, in the classroom, the teacher setting up a pairs exercise may place a strict limit on the time allowed, knowing that if a constraint is over-sustained the drama will disappear. At other times, however, the pairs may be 'empowered' to move the scene towards a more explicit mode of expression from one or more of the characters: the 'parent' of the late child 'loses' his/her temper in spite of the constraint; the grieving parents find a way of talking about the death of their daughter. For a dramatic playing exercise to include this 'change of gear' towards explicitness, and for it to be effective, the participants must be sensitive to both *when* and *how* to carry out this change. Obviously the transformation can only be a dramatic one if the experience of the constraint has been sufficient, both in terms of tension and duration.

The teacher of drama must help students to achieve the relevant skills of selecting, constructing and breaking constraints. These will in turn help the students to work on scripts, for the application of the notions of 'constraint' and 'breaking the constraint' will not only affect the way teachers and students prepare and reflect upon their dramatic playing exercises, it will also provide them with a new and interesting way of looking at written texts. One can 'hear' the restraint on both characters at the beginning of the following scene between Hamlet and his Mother:

HAMLET: Now, mother, what's the matter?
QUEEN: Hamlet, though hast thy father much offended.
HAMLET: Mother, you have my father much offended.
QUEEN: Come, come, you answer with an idle tongue.
HAMLET: Go, go, you question with a wicked tongue.

Both are testing the ground, both afraid of what will be said, of what will be done. But towards the end of the scene, as the rawness of the Queen's guilt and of Hamlet's contempt become exposed, they both lose hold of their constraint:

QUEEN: O Hamlet, speak no more.
Thou turn'st mine eyes into my very soul,
And there I see such black and grained spots
As will not leave their tinct.
HAMLET: Nay, but to live
In the rank sweat of an enseamed bed,
Stew'd in corruption, honeying and making love
Over the nasty sty!
QUEEN: O speak to me no more.
These words like daggers enter in my ears.
No more, sweet Hamlet.

Shakespeare, *Hamlet* Act III Scene IV

I have suggested that this kind of exercise, requiring pairs of pupils consciously to employ a constraint imposed by the teacher, is not suitable for young children. Many of them will already have an unconscious understanding of theatre form, observable in their 'free' play, but having to carry out a teacher-imposed 'constraint' task' is likely to be too much of a straight jacket for them.

This kind of knowledge about how theatre works can also be applied to pupils' illustrative/performance activities, where an interaction (that is, not a still picture) occurs between two or three participants. The teacher, working from the 'outside', can be actively engaged in going round the groups as they prepare their performances, or when the whole class is directing 'guinea pigs' at the front. S/he can prompt the participants to apply constraints on what the characters say to each other in order to make their work more theatrically exciting. When a performance is over the teacher can usefully lead a discussion about the validity of the kind of constraint (psychological, social, etc.) chosen by the characters, and the extent to which the 'audience' were made aware of the 'hidden truth' of the situation, in spite of the constraint. Of course, if the performance includes a character no longer able to sustain the constraint, such matters as the *timing* of the fracture, *how* it occurred and the *outcome* are all relevant matters for reflection. As I said earlier (p. 57), this kind of knowledge will also allow pupils to probe scenes from play-texts.

Manipulating time and space and other basic theatrical dimensions

When the class is operating as 'director', or there is small-group 'illustrative/performance' work going on, the teacher, working from 'the outside', can take the opportunity to teach about 'time and space' as dramatic dimensions. Such teaching is *always* conducted in terms of what the 'directors' or 'actors' are trying to say. The class is invited to experiment with how variation in the juxtaposition of the characters on stage in relation to distance, levels, light, colour and line can affect the *meaning* of what is being shown. Thus a teacher might typically ask, 'Does the audience sense anything different about this family if those two chairs are closer?', 'Is the evident constraint on this character likely to be made clearer if she doesn't answer his question straight away?', and so on.

Abstract movement

I mentioned in Chapter 2 (p. 26) how the use of 'alter egos' can become a form of theatre in its own right. Here again, not only can the teacher help the students to make a careful selection of the alter egos' dialogue, s/he can also open up all the exciting physical and spatial possibilities that having four actors to represent but two characters can offer.

Sometimes it will be appropriate for the teacher to introduce the pupils to a *dance* form. Because dance is more abstract than drama, it can help the performers and audience to capture the *essential* meaning of a dramatic situation. I have often invited my classes to discover what is *underneath* their actions and words by finding a *quality* of movement in space and a *relationship* in space that are non-naturalistic. A particular exercise I am fond of involves the participants (perhaps a group of four) sitting on chairs, close to each other. All but one of them are asked to express the inner feelings of the characters from a (very) short story, using their hands, arms and the angle of their heads only – no facial expression. The remaining member of the group narrates the story as they perform. This highly-disciplined form of theatre can be prepared by several small groups using the same story, so that as each is performed in turn the differences of interpretation can be enjoyed.

When I was working in Vancouver a couple of months ago, two of my Masters students adapted this exercise to the interpretation of a play-text. They deliberately chose the kind of condensed writing that amateur actors find difficult to handle. Hermia speaks first to Helen and then to Lysander:

> And in the wood, where often you and I
> Upon faint primrose beds were wont to lie,
> Emptying our bosoms of their counsel sweet,
> There my Lysander and myself shall meet;
> And thence from Athens turn away our eyes,
> To seek new friends, and stranger companies.
> Farewell, sweet playfellow; pray thou for us,
> And good luck grant thee thy Demetrius!
> Keep word, Lysander; we must starve our sight
> From lovers' food, till morrow deep midnight.
>
> Shakespeare, *A Midsummer Night's Dream* Act I Scene II

This exercise is characterised by the responsibilities it *removes* from the players: they are not required to *be* the characters, merely illustrations of them; they are not required to show feelings through the normal channel of facial expression, just through the quality of their hand and arm movements; they are not required to say their lines, a narrator carries that responsibility. They can both concentrate on the inner meanings of the text and enjoy expressing their interpretation through the limitations of restricted gesture. Again, it is useful to have several groups working on the same portion of text so that comparisons of interpretation can be appreciated.

This use of movement is effective because it is so restricted, using only hands, arms and heads in unison with poetic narration. There are many times, of course, when a teacher wants a class to experience freedom of movement. I should put 'freedom' in inverted commas because, of course, art is about finding parameters. Nevertheless, this implies full use of the body using all the dimensions of directness/indirectness, heaviness/lightness, sustaining/staccato, etc. available. So whether the children are to be toys that come to life, machines that take over the world, shades of the dead condemned eternally to the underworld, or Prometheus offering the gift of fire, they can explore different ways of moving in order to capture the essence of the story being told. This movement or dance form has an advantage over drama, in that it readily sheds the straight jacket of naturalism and gets to the heart of a theme at those times when anything less than poetic dialogue would reduce it to the banal.

Sitting-down drama

This is like going from the sublime to the ridiculous! Again, the participants are to be seated, but this time the whole class should be in a circle. The teacher controls what goes on 'from the outside'. You should appreciate that it is only under special circumstances that one should use this particular method (a point that is somewhat redundant as the previous approach equally requires special circumstances!). However, it should be understood that 'sitting-down' drama is more appropriate for the less intelligent group that may be hostile or reluctant about doing drama.

Like most of my best strategies in teaching I stumbled across this method when I found myself teaching in particularly demanding circumstances. I was doing drama in a psychiatric hospital with adult patients, most of whom looked as though they would rather run a mile than 'act'. So I invented the idea of 'making up a fictitious case-study of someone who had a huge problem'. *I* took the role of the person with the problem: 'What do you want the problem to be? . . . Do you want me to be a man or a woman? . . .', etc. The patients (a group of about ten) were to be people in the 'problem person's' life: family, authority figures, friends, etc. From there I proceeded to initiate the most low-key drama one could imagine. It was metaphorically as well as literally 'sitting down' – a kind of casual radio play where we just 'said what happened to come into our heads that might be the kind of thing people in this chap's life would say to him in connection with his problem'!

It is impossible here to describe the method in detail. What is important to understand is that the drama leader adopts the *opposite* attitude to what one normally expects of a drama initiator. S/he must be laid back, ready to laugh *with* them at some inappropriate contribution, forgetful, fumble for the words, uncertain as to what should be the next scene and constantly need the group to 'put him/her right'. The result in this case was, of course, that the group gradually took on a responsibility for the course of dramatic events and became absorbed in 'this chap's case-study'. Of course, in the hospital context, the problem I in role was invariably faced with matched that of one or more of the people in the group.

This procedure is almost 'anti-art'. It is banal in the extreme. I mention it here as an example of teaching objectives that have little to do with engaging the art form. Yet it had a powerful effect on the patients. They became intrigued by it. For some of them it was a chance to see their own problem operating at a distance from themselves; for others it was a chance to role-play 'other people', such as members of a family affected by a problem indirectly; for others it was a matter of power, to have a chance to manipulate someone else's life; or it was a matter of status, especially at the end of the session when they became a panel of consultants 'looking at' this man's case-study and advising on a course of treatment. Here the objectives were more to do with the self-esteem of members of the group than with subject matter or with theatre. It was a form of drama therapy.

Nevertheless I found myself, after the success of using this method occasionally in a hospital context, transferring it to educational and prison establishments. Sometimes I used it in the classroom with 'difficult' pupils. Again, it was noticeable how absorbed they became, provided I firmly signalled that we were not to take it seriously. In the school and prison situation, however, I did not take on the role of the protagonist myself, but asked for a volunteer. This was an interesting switch from the teacher working 'from the inside' to operating 'from the outside' with similar material. There is a significant difference between the *feel* of the two approaches. In working 'from the inside' one has a much greater chance of bringing credibility to the scenes and 'feeding' the other characters with dialogue they can respond to, another strength of T in R. Working 'from the outside' one can more easily operate as a commentator, weaving scenes together with narration and responding genuinely as a member of the audience.

In the school situation particularly, as the teacher proceeds with 'sitting-down' drama, s/he should look out for the opportunity to depart from it by moving into physical action, using spacial relationships rather than just 'voices'. In other words, such a method must be seen as a temporary phase on the way to drama proper. 'Sitting-down' drama is a device with severe limitations and should not be followed beyond its usefulness.

So far in this chapter I have looked at a number of ways in which a teacher can work as a fellow artist from 'outside' what is being created. I began by examining those kinds of pair or small-group exercises that can be directed towards either dramatic playing or illustrating/performance activity. It is important that neither the teacher nor the class confuses them. Both modes should employ in structuring a scene a key element of dramatic form: constraint. I proceeded to consider other theatrical elements, such as the manipulation of time and space, suggesting ways in which the teacher can *teach* for meaning-making in theatre when the members of the class are either preparing for showing in small groups or operating as 'directors' with a few selected 'guinea-pig' actors. I then moved to discussing two contrasted forms of drama, both of which, coincidentally, involved the participants sitting down. The first, using abstract movement, was essentially theatre; the second, 'sitting-down' drama, was a laid back, non-theatre activity used for promoting confidence in the participants. In the latter form the teacher could work either 'from the inside' (with psychiatric patients) or 'from the outside' (in an educational context).

The use of non-drama experience

It is often the case that a drama teacher turns to other forms of experience as part of a drama lesson or workshop. Games are very popular and are felt by many teachers to be necessary as 'warm-up' agents. There was a time in the early 1970s in England when one would come across schools in which a whole drama lesson was made up of such games. Games still form a very important part of drama work in many Canadian and American schools. As an inveterate course-attender myself I have participated whole-heartedly in such warm-ups, while really failing to see the point. But then, I tend to be sceptical about warm-ups generally, believing that working at any art creates its own warm-up. A painter does not warm-up first, nor does a playwright or a novelist, but then a dancer or a musician might! What I am sceptical of is *unfocused* warm-ups, a kind of unchannelled limbering up, which may often turn out to be inappropriate for the thing being created.

Now what I *am* keen on is the use of non-drama experiences that help create the right frame of mind, the right mood or the right atmosphere for the drama that is going to follow, or as a sequel to a drama that has just taken place. It might indeed be a game. For instance in setting up a drama with young adults about meeting secretly at a border crossing, I preceded it with a blindfold game in which partners could only recognise each other in a crowd from the feel of their hands. They had many moments of 'rejection' and 'frustration' before they found the right hands, and such 'relief' when they succeeded! Here the game is almost a microcosm of what was to follow in the dramatic fiction; it certainly created an appropriate mood.

There is a whole range of activities, not just games, that can be used to prepare for a drama exercise. Class discussion is about the most imprecise (but nevertheless sometimes necessary) method. 'Brainstorming' ideas on a particular topic also has its uses. Of particular use is to invite members of the class to walk in front of a large-size chart, map, diagram, list of quotations, blown-up extract from the text, etc. spread right across a classroom wall or covering a large floor or table-top. Having examined the display they can then add their own comments, query matters that do not seem clear and put their initials against matters they support. In the Salem work (p. 36), after brainstorming all the modern superstitions they could think of, I invited the class to go round each group's list (which were spread across the floor space) and initial those items of superstition that they could admit to being affected by. There is nothing quite like the act of putting one's name against something for generating a feeling of commitment. Those exercises that give specific sense experiences are more finely tuned towards entry into an art form. For instance: asking a class to make a collage of mysterious sounds as a way of creating the atmosphere for a drama to do with the underworld; to invoke images of a wall that is cold and dank to the touch as a preliminary to a 'cave' drama; to practise 'walking a tight-rope' for a circus drama; or to take young children out into the snow ready for both science and related dramatic work; or to visit a factory, a shopping mall or a railway station to pick information and impressions needed for their drama project.

I have also found invaluable the kind of movement work I learnt from the late Veronica Sherbourne (1990). In this approach, usually in pairs or very small groups, participants trustfully help each other to explore the capacity of their bodies for strength and submissiveness, in relation to each other and to the ground they are standing or lying on. Much of the work that we do in drama is dependent on trust: participants have to learn to trust the drama, the subject matter, the teacher, each other and, above all, to trust themselves. Veronica's work promotes the last two of these, giving everyone a sense of physical self, of at-oneness with others and a general sense of well-being. (Sherbourne, 1990). Here again I tend to extract exercises from her repertoire that will relate to whatever is needed in the drama, rather than offer my classes a regular diet of the work irrespective of what drama is to follow. So, for instance, if in pursuing the drama the students will need to acquire a respectful quality of touching each other, say in the emergency hospital set up in Atlanta, Georgia, during the Civil War, then I will use relevant movement exercises, or rather *experiences*. (Veronica once chided me for calling them exercises!)

Very occasionally I use movement work related to Laban's (1975) theory and practice. This approach was quite popular, particularly in the West Riding of Yorkshire, in the late 1960s in primary schools and with girls in

Secondary physical education. I have not seen much evidence of its use in recent years, but I still find it valuable as an introduction to characterisation and to the interpretation of texts. Linked with this is the wonderful approach to texts found in the work of Cecily Berry (1987).

Playwrighting

This activity is difficult to teach within the normal timetable of a school. It often benefits from the kind of extended workshops described by the late Gerald Chapman (1991). Nevertheless, opportunities for short-scene writing can occur in the classroom. I often set up an exercise where small groups create and write down a text which then has to be exchanged with another group for reinterpretation, rehearsal and performance. The following is such an example:

1. Introduce the circle game 'Keys of the Kingdom', in which a blindfold person, sitting on the floor in the middle of the circle, tries to guard the keys from the members forming the circle who want to snatch them away.
2. Once the rules are understood, have several small groups play the game spread around the room.
3. Discuss the principles underlying the game, then 'brainstorm' ways in which 'real-life' situations might parallel the game.
4. Ask each group to make *and rehearse* a short scene (no more than four lines of dialogue) that has a similar 'feel' and similar rules to the game.
5. When they have rehearsed to their satisfaction, that is so that the scene rings 'true' for them, instruct them to write down the dialogue and then pass their script on to another group.
6. When each group has a new script, have them cast, rehearse and, in turn, *perform* it to the rest of the class.
7. Discuss the interpretation after each performance. *Additionally*, have the *writers* perform their own script as they had originally intended it to be played.

This kind of exercise (with older adolescents and adults) has the objective of opening up what we mean by 'interpretation' in respect of three activities: reading, writing and performing a script.

5 Planning a Sequence of Drama Experiences

I established in Chapter 2 (p. 11) that one of the assumptions I work on is that drama is primarily about making social contexts. Another major assumption is that the teacher sees drama as *being about something that matters.* The intention is to engage with some aspect of life using dramatic form. This does not imply just *one* dramatic form. Rather, understanding is likely to be enriched by experiencing a sequence of different kinds of activities. These may include dramatic playing, different forms of illustrative/performance activity, other art forms, scripts, direct experiences, movement, games, discussion and library research. The teacher envisages an accumulation of understanding through a series of 'steps'. Some examples of these steps and the thinking behind them are examined in this chapter. Let me reiterate, they are *examples*, not models!

The moment one starts to think about planning a drama experience one's concern is not only with content and how best to set up some kind of learning. Attention should also be given to the degree of autonomy the participants are to have within the experience. There are several levels of such autonomy:

1 The class chooses the topic.
2 The class takes over and changes the direction of the drama part-way through.
3 The class has considerable room to manoeuvre without changing the thrust of the learning area.
4 The only opportunity for individual invention lies within strict parameters, laid down at each step in the sequence.
5 There is no student autonomy at all.

These classifications *seem* to go from freedom of choice to virtually no choice at all. In fact it is not as straightforward as that, for although in following category 1 the teacher, having heard the topic chosen, may still be rigidly manipulative, and in category 4 the participants may feel manipulated without realising that the parameters release them into creativity, we are often at our most creative when the boundaries are clearly drawn for us. That is not to deny that as teachers we may at times be guilty of being under or over-restrictive. No doubt it is part of every teacher's style to err towards one or the other. My own tendency is towards over-restriction. This may be because of the peculiar one-off circumstances in which I tend to teach. It is noticeable that when I was teaching full-time I offered my own students greater freedom of choice than I allow other people's!

The key factor is *time*. When one is continually working with a group for a limited time, one feels impelled to adopt a style of preparation that will *guarantee* some kind of worthwhile experience; 'selling' drama to a reluctant class of students; 'selling' drama to a sceptical group of watching teachers; making sure the class learns something in the short time allowed; demonstrating a particular method to a group of interested professionals; making dramatic playing work for a group of students or teachers whom one suspects have been brought up on a diet of illustrative/performance drama. Working under these kinds of pressure often leads me to eschew student initiative and press for other ways of helping the class to feel they have had a worthwhile experience. The sense of well-being that comes to a class from having taken a major responsibility in the decision-making process tends to be left out, except *within* a particular step. So, for instance, in working on the theme of Orwell's *Nineteen Eighty-four*, I decided that we should use the character of Mrs. Parsons (Winston Smith's apartment neighbour) as a microcosm of the whole book, *I* chose the extract from the text for close analysis, *I* decided that the class should create a sculpture to capture the 'essence' of that extract, *I* decided that Mrs. Parsons should be sent for by the Thought Police to be questioned about what she had observed of her neighbour's movements, etc. *But* members of the class had freedom to try out their own method of text analysis, their own form of sculpture and to set up the interrogation in any way they liked. This seems to me to be a perfectly valid way of working. It falls somewhere between Categories 3 and 4 above. The class may have felt heavily manipulated in that they had no say in the direction of the lesson, nor in the choice of 'step' at any point in the sequence. However, judging by the energy put into these experiences and the quality of work by groups with whom I have used this sequence, the very 'tightness' of the 'givens' stimulated the creativity. (You don't experience satisfaction every time you use a particular piece of material with a group, nor can you always put your finger on why something did not work. For example I once tried the same Orwell sequence with a group of Leicester teachers who seemed to get no satisfaction from it whatsoever.)

The huge advantage of this planned, sequential way of working is that a steady course towards a *coherent* experience, both conceptually and artistically, is more likely to be achieved. The more choice the class is given, the greater the risk that a myriad decisions are being made by members of the class without the overall view of the work that the teacher holds. Let me hasten to say that it is sometimes appropriate for such a risk to be taken, for on occasion class autonomy has priority over any other goal. Even so, one should never hand over autonomy lightly. Indeed, I am not sure that 'hand over' is an appropriate metaphor: autonomy is not something to be 'given' by a teacher to his/her pupils; it is something to be '*earned*' by them. I believe there to be a class 'readiness' for autonomy, especially in respect of the dramatic playing activity. It has to do with the degree of commitment, ownership, trust and resources observable in the group as a whole. Autonomy can lie uneasily with a class whose social dynamics are destructive, or for whom, for a number of reasons, the theme is not yet accessible.

I have described the particular kind of pressures in my own work that push me in the direction of tight structuring. More often than we think, a classroom teacher or drama teacher in a Secondary school is similarly pressed into tight structuring, but perhaps for different reasons. The following examples illustrate some of these reasons:

1 I was working recently with teachers in Austria whose Drama timetable was rigidly 50 minutes a week. Under such circumstances the teacher must have a firm hold on the reins if the pupils are to have a significant experience. If, as I believe, the best kind of work emerges when a theme is sustained over many hours of work, this can only be achieved if the teacher is a wizard at re-stimulating interest in the most economical way at the beginning of each 50-minute session.

2 Another reason for careful structuring arises from what it is that is to be learnt. As I am fond of saying, 'If you are using drama to teach Road Safety, then that is what your pupils must finish up understanding'. Offering your young children choices of a fundamental kind will be out of place, although, of course, they may have the responsibility to make decisions at a superficial level, such as choosing the name for the imaginary boy or girl who is going to break the Road Safety code in the story. (This is exactly what I did with a class of six-year olds when I was asked to teach Road Safety). Such a decision will be very important to the children in terms of their 'owning' their created protagonist, but will not, of course, affect the direction of the teaching. Again there will

be an opportunity for spontaneous dialogue with the children: 'I'm sorry to bother you', I said, using T in R with the children as 'neighbours', 'but I'm worried about Michael . . . He hasn't come home from school . . . Is he playing with any of your children? . . . Would you mind looking? . . . What could have happened? . . .', and so on. In this way the teacher controls direction, but s/he does not know *how* the news of Michael's accident will emerge. This, it seems to me, is what is meant by careful planning. It even allows for the children to take over the scene about hunting for Michael, but, significantly, the children are in a position only to 'own' what the teacher has offered for 'sale'. I chose to impose a focus of seeing a road accident through the eyes of an anxious parent. This structure remains unchangeable, whatever the children do with it. In other words, it is not merely that thc teacher imposes a theme, 'Road Safety', but s/he also imposes the theatre form through which that theme is to be experienced. This particular lesson is discussed further in Chapter 6 (p. 112).

3 Another kind of occasion when the teacher uses tight structuring occurs when the class needs convincing that the teacher knows what s/he is doing. Students who are sceptical of drama, or who are embarrassed by it, need to feel safe in this teacher's hands. This often means having the security of a clear teacher-plan. Incidentally, I often share with my classes what that plan is, indicating the different kinds of demands that will be required of them, perhaps even warning them that certain sections will 'be rather tricky', 'be a bit boring', or 'require hard thinking', or even: 'When we come to the middle section of the lesson we shall need to put our heads together on how best to do it – I'm not sure . . .'.

4 A sureness of 'teacher touch' must also be in evidence when the theme or topic is a delicate one. It is no use inviting an inexperienced drama class to discuss how they should do drama about AIDS! When I undertook such a theme I could almost hear the sigh of relief from the students, who had eagerly asked for the subject when my lesson began, as I divided them into groups of four and instructed, 'Now that our firm is beginning to have a reputation for forward thinking, we have been asked to design a hospice for AIDS patients . . .'. Having been scared at the prospect of what we were going to tackle, they suddenly felt safe in the role of designers. This allowed them to risk talking to each other seriously about the needs of such patients, and gradually helped them to feel secure enough to move into being 'in role' as the patients them-

> selves. No way can a teacher expect a class to come up with its own ideas for its own protection. Because the subject is an emotive one the students are dependent on the *teacher's* maturity, professionalism and knowledge of drama to ease them into handling it.

In spite of all these valid reasons for a teacher keeping a firm control over the drama sequence, s/he must be continually alert for opportunities to 'hand over power' to his/her students. If they too are to work as artists, they must build confidence in their own ability to make drama themselves. As I suggested above (p. 65), the extent of such autonomy will vary from decision-making within a short step of a sequence to having overall responsibility for a whole experience. Let me make it clear that this has nothing to do with the age of the participants. Given the right circumstances, four-year olds are capable of making major decisions about the substance or direction of the drama, while a group of adults might conceivably be judged as 'not ready'.

It is now time to look at some sequences in detail. The first two examples are drawn from recent practice with adult teachers, using material adapted from my work with children of different ages. Because I am often required to do workshops with teachers, I try to devise work that can operate in this way at many levels. I do this on the assumption that the *principles* behind the planning are the same, and, although the main purpose is to give the teachers something to transfer to their own classroom contexts, they can nevertheless enjoy the dramatic material at their own adult level.

It is probably necessary at this point to explain the layout of the lesson sequences that are to follow. The first point I want to make is that you should not attempt to read the sequences through as a continuous reading exercise. Rather, I suggest you 'dip in', picking whatever sequence currently interests you. Otherwise a combination of boredom and indigestion is likely to set in!

There are two parts to the text. The first (serif typeface) gives a brief description of what occurred, the 'plot' of the sequence, as it were. The second (sans serif typeface) offers an explanation or commentary, often bringing out certain teaching points. I hope the division of the text in this way is helpful.

Robin Hood
(with nine/ten-year olds and adults)

Step 1

I explained to the adult class that they were going to work on the above theme (using a sequence of steps close to, but not the same as, the work I did with nine-year olds some time ago). 'I appreciate that the prospect of representing Medieval times might seem daunting, but it will be my responsibility to make it work for you.'

Notice the importance of sharing with a class that you understand some of their likely apprehensions.

Step 2

'In pairs, tell each other (not 'in role') how you think arrows were made in Robin Hood's day. What kind of wood? What size? How heavy? What was the head made of? . . . and so on. Where you don't know, just guess.' When they had finished I invited them to accept, for the time being, all their shared suppositions and guesses as *facts*.

This is a light-hearted, very narrowly focused 'way in' to the drama. Some students automatically use their notebooks to draw diagrams as they explain things to each other.

'In the same pairs, give an exaggerated version of a contemporary Professor of History giving his annual lecture on how they made arrows in Medieval times, one of you in role as the professor, the other as the professor's class of students – who may of course ask questions!'

Again, this is very much a tongue-in-cheek exercise, but it gives the first taste of being 'in role'. It releases lots of laughter from some of the adults. I would not, of course, choose to do this part of the step with nine-year olds.

'In the same pairs, you are now ('in role') father and son living in Medieval times, with the father teaching the son how to make arrows.' This needs setting up more elaborately and will only work if the students achieve a fair degree of concentration. Before they start it is necessary for the 'father' to define his space: 'Stand in front of your bench where you are intending to work. See it in your mind's eye. Touch it. Know its dimensions. Know what tools are on it in preparation for arrowmaking and exactly where everything is. When you feel you "know" your workbench, call your son in.'.

This is a first taste of dramatic playing to be taken seriously. Some of the adults may not be able to manage it. On one occasion, described in Chapter 2 (p. 14), one pair discovered dried flower stalks which *initially* helped them to believe in what they were doing. Gradually, however, these 'props' became an obstacle to true creativity. This is quite a difficult exercise for inexperienced role-players for, even if belief in the 'arrow' is not a stumbling block, there is a chance that they will fall down on the 'father-son' relationship. For these reasons the exercise is very helpful to the teacher diagnostically, for you can soon spot which members of the class are likely to contribute positively and which are likely to need more help.

It is often useful to warn inexperienced people that, in doing an exercise of this kind, they will not all finish at the same time. You should instruct them to rely on themselves for deciding when it is not productive to continue, and to sit quietly watching the others.

Afterwards, encourage discussion of how the students fared in the exercises. You could compare the kind of language register used in each part of the exercise, noticing how the 'here and now' feel of the last one is supported by physical actions and paralinguistic gestures.

Step 3

'We are now going to build a Medieval Nottinghamshire village – a village of craftsmen. Each family, a group of five or six, will be responsible for a different craft. Having started this session concentrating on *arrows,* I am now going to ask you to suspend the idea of being arrowmakers for the time being. All will be made clear as we proceed, you'll just have to take it on trust! So, each "family" choose a craft. When we have heard what you have chosen, I will ask you to work out a way of using each member of your family in a different part of the process. If, for example, you choose weaving, then one person teases out the wool, another washes it, another takes the dry wool for spinning, another sets up the weaving frame, etc. Practise these tasks separately. When you are familiar with the miming actions, don't attempt to make it a naturalistic interaction with dialogue, just work at it as a task to be demonstrated to an audience. Start to plan a kind of "moving collage" in silent mime of a whole family at work. Create the overall rhythm of the 'picture' in one circular motion. When we see each group's performance in turn we should be able to guess what each member of your family is doing. We might also be able to guess which of you is the "head of the family".'

This is a huge shift from working in pairs, but notice again that it tightly focuses the students' attention on a 'projected' activity, that is on outside actions rather than on themselves. Yet it should be highly disciplined, with the teacher using words and phrases like 'collage', 'demonstrate', 'performance', 'we should be able to guess', etc. That it is to be non-naturalistic and illustrative is a protection – the students are not being asked to *be* those families, merely to demonstrate physical actions. *But* there is plenty of opportunity for free chat among themselves as they work out how they are going to portray their craft. Leaders will emerge. The atmosphere should be one of energetic enjoyment.

Step 4

The presentations were seen in turn, creating a context of a 'living museum', with the rest of the class as the general public. We then went through a process of 'showing', audience response and feedback from the actors. I reminded the students that the purpose of the exercise was to give both an overall aesthetic picture of a harmonious, rhythmic craft process and sufficient clear detail for the audience to recognise the nature of each person's task.

It cannot be overemphasised how useful it is to make an important occasion of this kind of presentation, partly out of respect for the actors, and partly as a way of making sure that those in the 'audience' understand that *they* have a responsibility; *they* have to work at their interpretation of what they see. For this reason I will often signal a point when the audience may break off from merely watching and switch to whispering to each other what they are observing, *then* proceed to make their thoughts public.

Step 5

'Now we shall move into a dramatic playing activity. All the families will carry on working but, instead of 'showing' the work to someone, it will actually be happening. You may talk to each other quietly as you work if you wish. Let us assume that it is noon on a hot summer's day, so that you are either working outside your houses or at least with all windows and doors thrown open. Then it will be easy for you to see a stranger arriving: first the sound of horse's hoofs and then, when he appears, you will see from his apparel that he is one of Robin Hood's men. I shall play the stranger but, instead of suddenly appearing, I shall start to 'narrate' his entrance. I shall say something like: "Absorbed in their tasks they were surprised to realise they had a visitor ... They did not know him, but recognised ...", and so on. I will then start interacting with you.'

Notice this way of introducing T in R, both warning that it will happen and explaining what form it will take, that is using narration preceding direct speech. I did not make this elaborate preparation with the nine-year old children, I simply burst in 'in role'. One has to sense which method will work best for the particular class. No doubt with inexperienced adolescents I would resort to paving the way as I did for these adults.

I arrived 'in role' and apologetically explained, 'Robin Hood needs urgent assistance with a supply of arrows as he proposes to attack Nottingham castle where two of his men are imprisoned. Could you drop your normal crafts for a while and help Robin Hood out by making arrows instead?' I intimated that I would give them time to think it over.

Thus the teacher imposes the beginnings of a 'plot' which, s/he knows, will have a further twist when s/he arrives later in his/her second role, as a representative from the sheriff inviting the villagers to show their craft at the Sheriff's annual fair. This imposition of a dilemma is a classic use of T in R and is useful if employed occasionally. Overdone, it loses its effectiveness.

When I put Robin Hood's request to the nine-year olds they wanted to give a promise to the stranger straight away. For the adults this, not unexpectedly, became a concern about economics and where one's duty lay. Holding a discussion is the first taste of informal talk 'in role' and is quite a test for both adolescents and adults. Their grip on their roles and their belief in the fictitious context is very slender for, after all, all they have done so far is to imitate actions of carrying out a craft. So this is a big leap towards 'ownership'. The teacher must not expect too much and be tolerant of giggling and other out-of-role indications. This is one of the points where the *time factor* makes an enormous difference. If you are under pressure to 'pursue a quick dramatic experience' then you will follow the steps as described here. If, however, there is plenty of time it would be appropriate at this point to evolve a series of steps gradually leading to a deeper understanding of their economic situation. This can be done by establishing how their goods were marketed, whether there was any surplus income, etc., so that the wider implications of giving up a few days to make arrows for Robin Hood are fully appreciated before they make their decision.

Step 6

I as T in R as a representative from the Sheriff: 'You will be honoured to hear that your village has been chosen to show its craft wares at the coming Sheriff's Nottingham Fair!'.

When I did this with adults they became concerned about the effect this kind of political pressure could have on a community. Families that had been in harmony started, through disagreement about the issue, to break up, father against son, etc. Also, individual families drew apart.

It is worth considering in some detail the differences that have occurred in using the same material with different adult groups. When I was doing a workshop in Columbus, Ohio, I followed the sequence as I have described it above, but I did not use the arrival of a messenger from the Sheriff as the class took the work in a direction that rendered such a step unnecessary. I did however introduce the following further steps.

Step 7

I interrupted their reaction to the message from Robin Hood, noting the direction of their discussion which mentioned matters like 'being stone-masons working on the new Cathedral'. I asked them in their family groups very quickly (it had to be done speedily so that the storyteller would in part extemporise) to make up a story of some past incident that enhanced Robin Hood's reputation as a hero in the eyes of the family, the kind of story that might well be told today in Northern Ireland, Iraq or America of recent 'successful' exploits. 'Select from your family a "storyteller" who will now proceed to tell the whole village, sitting on the floor, as children soaking up the heroic tale.' (This gives status to the teller and the tale.)

Step 8

I then talked about the new Cathedral to be built in the Nottingham Priory, *their chief customer*, the abbott of the priory, being a friend of the Sheriff! I asked them in their families to draw the design of their craft – appropriate, of course, to the Cathedral or Priory. As they drew their designs they moved into their roles of reacting to Robin Hood's messenger. They then opened the exercise up into a 'village discussion'. It became clear that all the families were prepared to support the outlaw's cause, but precautions had to be taken. One family mentioned regular visits by the Sheriff's men. This, of course, gave me a clue for subsequent 'steps', to 'cover up' the arrowmaking.

Step 9

I asked them in their families (but 'out of role') to discuss 'what a perceptive observer might notice about what was going on'.

Step 10

I then asked for one volunteer from each family to play the role of a sheriff's recorder (or spy!). The volunteers then 'visited' each family and asked questions, *without actually accusing.*

Notice that not actually accusing is more dramatic; it is a form of constraint: to reach a point of *explicit* accusation weakens the drama.

Step 11

Following the above small-group dramatic playing, the next step found a way of elevating the interaction to whole group 'theatre'. I took on the role of the Sheriff's representative to whom the 'visitors' had to report. *But* the 'reporting' took place in front of the family houses, with the families lined up to hear and defend the suspicions of the 'visitors'. I used my role to create a sense of order and of the Sheriff's huge authority over these people. They struggled impressively to defend themselves, a strong 'community' feel growing in the process. This was exciting stuff! When we (the Sheriff's people) departed, the drama was over, but of course there was a lot to talk about, not least the powerful theatrical note on which we had finished.

Just two days later in New York, another adult group handled similar material quite differently. I also made some amendments. I decided not to start the work with the arrowmaking exercise but to wait until I thought it was *needed.* So we began with the 'craft collage' and then moved to the arrival of the messenger from Robin Hood, after which I introduced the 'storytelling' and imposed the idea that Prince John, Robin Hood's enemy, was their main customer. On the messenger's return, each family agreed to find some way of making arrows. 'If you play your cards right you could earn royal patronage that will stay with your family for future generations!' *At this point I put them in pairs, with one family member explaining to the other how to make arrows.* Then I got them to shift gradually from *explaining* the process to actually carrying it out. I *then* took the role of the Sheriff's man inviting them to have their wares on display at the Sheriff's forthcoming exhibition. It was at this point that I left them to it for the whole-group dramatic playing acquired considerable energy, commitment and absorption related to whether one particular family could be trusted. After more than twenty minutes, I interrupted and suggested we brought the work to a close. Their animated discussion revealed that one family was indeed working for Prince John. So I finished with an exercise in which each member of that family, now twenty years on, was faced with two or three 'children' (the rest of the class') pursuing the question 'What did you do for our hero Robin?'. When this 'closure' was over I filled in some historical background related to King Richard's capture and high taxes to pay ransom money.

These two pieces of work relating to Robin Hood took on totally contrasting dramatic forms. It seems to me both are valid. This reinforces my point that the examples of sequences in this chapter must not be taken as patterns to be followed, but as indicators of the notion of logical progression within a process. This logic can take many different forms. With the nine-year olds the Robin Hood exercise became a game of 'hiding arrows from the sheriff's man', who gradually became more suspicious that all was not what it seemed. When he finally challenged them, one family threw in the hint that the village had the plague! (A nice example of working within the logic of the social context.)

It is interesting to consider what learning the nine-year old children might have gained during the Robin Hood sequence. It is possible that they learnt about:

- arrows and a chosen craft;
- that period of history: the power of a sheriff; what it was to be an outlaw; the political strife between Richard the Lionheart and King John;

- decision-making;
- working as a family group;
- the skills of selectivity in portraying an action with care;
- identifying the logic behind a problem posed by the T in R;
- being forced to deceive and disguise one's true attitude.

The drama can open up any of these areas of learning for members of the class. Not all students will be engaged with all of the items listed and some may remain untouched by everything. (The child whose mind the whole time is on getting home to her birthday party is unlikely to learn very much.) Insight into any aspect of the above areas is unlikely to occur without the chance of *reflection*. Aspects like the last in the list, especially, will stay at a pleasurable game level unless the teacher can help the pupil to look at the implications of the 'game' and apply them to other contemporary and, perhaps, personal situations. The art form creates the 'gut' experience; it is never explicit in what it teaches; it 'opens up' possibilities of things partially sensed, often related to values that are half-understood. Unless there is reflection – and this is where the teacher can help – through the sharing of feelings and thoughts ('discussion' is too arid for what I mean), and through other art forms like poetry, painting, etc., the chance to 'get' what has been elusive can be lost. I deliberately use the colloquial term 'get', for it involves a kind of understanding with one's whole being, a eureka!: 'I *get* it!'. The art experience offers this gut-level kind of understanding. This is why it is superior to the intellectualising that schools are mostly concerned with.

Croft
(with older adolescents and adults)

This sequence uses the poem 'Croft', by Stevie Smith, as a starting point.

Step 1

'The poem I am about to write on the blackboard has only four lines. For a bit of fun I'm just going to write the first three and see if you can guess the last':

Aloft
In the loft
Lies Croft ...
?

'Talk to your neighbour and, if you like, write down your last line. Any suggestions?'

This is a 'fun' way of getting a class to give close attention to the poem. Discussion of the significance of the repeated 'oft's' may be useful; on the other hand it is much better, on hearing the class's last lines, to draw attention to the way 'oft' has been used in the suggestions. Make sure there is something to commend each one.

Step 2

I added the final line:

He is soft

Then I invited them to comment on whether this line was an improvement on their inventions.

'From the poem we are collectively, to begin with, going to create an agreed image of Croft. Please bear in mind that we are creating a *person* – I have to insist on this for the sake of the work to follow. What kind of images come into your heads?' Brainstorming followed: loneliness, aloneness, fear, hiding, softness, cowardice, backward, not right in the head, etc. 'Can we have a volunteer "guinea-pig" to act as Croft? The class will direct you. We are going to consider what we want the audience to see when the curtain goes up. Croft will be alone in the loft. What instructions can you give our 'actor' so that the audience immediately picks up vibes about the kind of images you have been suggesting.'

This use of the class having a 'director's' eye is a very useful way of working. If there appeared to be a lot of differences of opinion I would ask the class to split into small groups, and ask each group to create a 'Croft image' for us all to respond to. Decisions have to be taken about whether he is to stand sit or lie, about the angle of his body and limbs, about his clothing and the way he wears things (for instance a shoelace undone or one shoe off), and about any properties (one group wanted Croft to have a teddy bear, with a well-chewed paw in his mouth).

Step 3

I explained that this next phase would need complicated instructions, part of the purpose being to break the 'stereotype' inevitably established. I divided the class into groups of eight or ten (it must be an even number). With one adult group I asked them to prepare a choral speaking of the poem at this point, using their 'Croft' as a central image, before going on to the following tasks.

Each group considered who the characters were who lived in the same house as Croft. They discussed contrasting attitudes that Croft's family might have towards him. In their groups of eight, four members were cast as *four* of those characters.

Each family character took a partner from the rest of the group who was to be Croft. Thus there were four family members, *each* with a 'Croft'. Each pair then discussed how the particular family member *'saw'* Croft, and the actor playing Croft created that image. In other words, what was to be shown to the audience were four *versions* of Croft, each one according to a different family member's perspective.

Not surprisingly, even an adult class will struggle with what is required here. We are so used to 'creating' our own characters, based on our inner experience of them, that having to adapt to someone else's perspective seems at first to be perplexing. But once the group gets the idea, it becomes an appealing one. The teacher needs to go round checking that all pairs have understood what is required of them.

Step 4

Continuing with the above, I interrupted their preparations to demand a further dimension. Once each pair had 'got it right', the whole group was instructed to create a *collage* of four versions of Croft. They were to arrange the eightsome in any way that looked interesting, seeing the juxtaposition of these contrasted versions from the audience's point of view.

Step 5

The 'showing' to the rest of the class adopted the method mentioned in the Robin Hood sequence. *But* I then said, 'I'm going to ask you all to redo the collage, but this time you will prepare a line of dialogue to be spoken by each member of the family to each 'Croft'. This line should be one that you feel stems from the attitude struck and which is typically said by that character to Croft. In your groups, *rehearse* the sequence of these four lines, giving due attention to the sense of theatre in the presentation. *However,* when you first resume your positions, each member of the *audience* will write down his/her guess as to what that line of dialogue might be. When they have shared their guesses with you, *then* you will give them the full performance.'.

This is an example of the audience being *actively* engaged.

What you do now will depend very much on the direction the class appears to be taking. The three groups in my adolescent class seemed, with the exception of one or two characters in each family, to emphasise the *burden* that Croft laid on the family. So, for instance, we discussed the extent to which frustration, anger and guilt featured. For example: 'Does the elder sister, who always has to 'baby-sit' with Croft, hide or show her frustration?'.

When I did this work with a New York University class, however, I suggested that we should look at Croft in terms of the handicapped child having power over other members of his family. First I proceeded to set up a movement experience with the class, based on Veronica Sherbourne's work (1990) where, in pairs, members of the class could use pushing, leaning and head support exercises to look at energy and the source of physical power. This exercise finished with Croft's 'parent' gently cradling Croft.

I asked each 'Croft' to find a space in the room that could become Croft's loft. Each 'parent' ('out of role') then watched his/her 'Croft' ('in role') play there.

I then set up a sustained dramatic playing experience, to be played almost 'at life rate', during which the unwilling parent was to climb up the steps to the loft. Here s/he would tell Croft that in future the loft was to be used for another purpose (the two actors beforehand had to agree on the kind of legitimate reason, such as a sick younger sibling). During the scene the parent was to become defeated and 'know' that Croft had the upper hand. The scene finished when the resigned parent descended the steps.

This is an example of existential interaction within very strictly defined parameters. This kind of exercise requires integrity and considerable concentration.

Each pair analysed what had happened in their scene. Then they described the scene to another pair. This new foursome now *chose* one of the two scenes and turned the incident in the loft into an abstract theatre piece, refined and carefully rehearsed, using the four actors as the two characters and their alter egos or narrators.

This is a demanding, disciplined and exciting exercise which, at every step, requires the participants to probe the meaning of power in a relationship. In this case the group comprised experienced adults. With adolescents one *might*, alternatively, turn to an established text rather than ask them to create their own. The discussions that follow the work with adolescents guide the teacher both in seeing how deeply the class are dealing with the issue and towards what the next steps should be. If the work has kept its 'centre', then something that pursues how a family is affected by a problem child (with or without reference to Croft) would seem appropriate. The text of both Peter Nicholl's *A Day in the Death of Joe Egg* and Cecil Taylor's *Operation Elvis* are suitable.

The adolescent class with whom I did this work sustained their interest in the central theme of a child as a burden to some selfish and influential members of a family, but our time was running out. I chose to set up a pairs exercise to round the work off. One student was in role as Croft, the other as the member of the family chosen to tell Croft that he was to go away to a residential home. The participants had to decide *who*, in the family they had been in, would be chosen to carry out this delicate task – for example the one who was genuinely fond of Croft, or the one who could dissemble best? Thus the work finished as a dramatic playing activity, with many of the participants taking on a different role from that they had played previously.

This is an occasion, which occurs quite frequently, where theme has priority over role. The whole of the sequence was about engaging with a central issue, rather than with 'building a character'. Teachers who have been trained to put their faith in getting their students to 'build characters' will find this thematic approach untenable. That is not to say that it would never be appropriate to spend a whole sequence examining a particular character or characters, but then *that* would become the theme!

The Nativity
(witn six/seven-year olds)

The class had asked to do drama about the Nativity – it was just before Christmas.

Step 1

I asked whether we could agree that this was Bethlehem and that our house was in 'the space over there' (the other end of the hall). I told them that, at first, I was going to be a stranger arriving in Bethlehem.

Step 2

With the children seated in a group on the floor I entered as Joseph, supporting a weary Mary. 'It's all right my dear, I'm sure we'll find somewhere to stay the night ... You rest here awhile and I'll ask these people ...'.

The role of Mary was established simply by the 'supportive' way I was holding my arm. Once I had sat her down on a chair in front of the children I came out of role.

'What have you seen so far? Is there a scarf that we could use as Mary's head covering, so that we know she's sitting here?' Not surprisingly they found a blue one which I draped over the back of the chair. Then, into role again, 'Excuse me ... My wife and I have travelled all the way from Nazareth ... Her baby is expected tonight ... Could we stay in your house? ...'. They immediately agreed. I came out of role again and explained that I was going to be someone else, '... and he's not going to be very pleased.'.

Notice this 'out of role' warning to the class, given with a wry smile, indicating that it is going to be both tough and yet fun.

Step 3

Coming from 'our house' in my new role I said, 'Who's that you have been talking to? ... I hope you haven't invited them to supper ... They're staying the *night*! ... She's having a *baby*! ... But that means we'll have to look after her ... I don't know anything about babies, and I'm sure you don't'. The children protested and I responded, 'They have to be washed and powdered, and all sorts of things you know nothing about ... I bet you don't even know how to pick a baby up ...' (They protested further.) '... All right, show me ... Imagine you've all got a baby in front of you ... I bet you can't pick it up gently enough ...' (They demonstrated with ease!). Then grudgingly I said, 'Well anyone can do that, but I bet you can't take its nappy off without hurting it ...', and so on, including bathing, powdering, putting a clean nappy on, feeding and rocking to sleep. So in the end I agreed that we knew enough to house the strangers. 'What did you say their names were?!'

Notice this aggressive style of T in R. Used sparingly, children enjoy the confrontation game. It gives them an enormous feeling of success because they always win in the end!

Step 4

We all walked into the house and sat in a circle. The scarf was in the middle to mark where Mary was lying on the bedding of straw we had given her. I asked them to close their eyes as I proceeded to tell the story of the birth: 'That night was a very special night ... The kind people who had taken Mary in waited while the baby was born.'. As I made sure they all had their eyes closed, I reached for the scarf and folded it in my arms, baby-shaped. 'It seemed a long wait. When it first started to get light they went into the room. There they saw the baby wrapped in a blue shawl.' 'Out of role' I said, 'Open your eyes.'. Then, back 'in role', 'This baby ...' (holding it up) '... has been born in our house. Shall we give it a name?'.

'Jesus!', they affirmed.

I then started a ceremony, saying something like, 'I name this baby, Jesus', then passed the 'child' on to the nearest pupils, who said something similar and passed it on, right round the circle. The final child then gave it back to its 'mother', and we sang 'Silent Night'.

This shows the importance of ritual in drama and is a very good example of the existential mode of *experiencing*.

Content and form are 'at one' here: using a number of theatrical devices (symbol, ritual, narrative, miming simple tasks, etc.) the central theme of the ordinariness and extraordinariness of this event is experienced.

The 'Vegetable'

(with older adolescents)

I have chosen this example because the theme happens to be, in many ways, close to that of the Croft exercise, and yet the sequence of drama experiences is quite different. The theme, 'distraught members of a family after the son has been badly injured in a car accident', was taken from a British Columbia Theatre Arts syllabus: 'Topics for Improvisations'. (The Theatre Arts students were seventeen-year olds.)

Step 1

'In pairs, one of you tell the other about a road accident that happened either to you or someone you know.'

This is a 'comfortable' way of starting on a theme and is also useful diagnostically. The next step is, of course, much more demanding.

Step 2

'Now, the "listener". You are to retell that same story to your partner, *as though it had happened to you*, and the 'new' listener is to receive it with respect.'

Step 3

'May we hear one or two of those accounts?'

This is a challenge and the teacher is taking a risk for, if this is to be done at all, it has to be done well enough to set the tone of seriousness that the theme requires.

I chose the most poignant one and asked, 'Is the original 'teller' prepared to answer further questions about what happened?'. We pulled our chairs into a tight circle and the group was invited to ask questions, in a way that respected the feelings of the one whose incident it was.

This brings home to the class that drama is about 'real' events that have an impact on people. Had we not conducted these preliminary steps, my guess is that the class would have indulged in typically glib improvisation.

After a further account from another pupil, I invited someone to tell a story with a 'lighter' tone. Lots of release of laughter followed.

This appears to contradict what I said above, but in fact it teaches that 'there is a time to be serious and a time to laugh', and that which of those times we are in will be made clear throughout the drama work!

Step 4

I then set two chairs in front of the class's semicircle of chairs and said, 'I'm going to begin the improvisation, but you are not going to play the part; you are going to *represent* the parents, Mr and Mrs Johnson, in thought.'.

I, teacher-in-role as a hospital doctor, invited two imaginary parents to sit on the chairs. I explained to the 'parents' that their son would need immediate surgery and that, if successful, he may fully recover, die or regress to a vegetable state. The members of the class from their semicircle asked questions *as if* they were the two people sitting on the chairs in front of the doctor.

Notice this convention of a 'collective voice'. This is a 'dramatic' episode inviting the worst possible kind of 'soap' pseudo-hysterics from the two 'parents'. By having the class collectively responsible for asking the questions, and by having the teacher talking to two empty chairs, everyone's minds are focused on the appropriateness of the questions and answers, *not* on the emotional state of the parents. This is a good example of a hybrid form between dramatic playing and illustrative/performance activity. The stylised form controls the interactions to such an extent that it becomes abstract theatre.

Step 5

There are often choices to be made about where the class want to take the Drama. So, out of role, it is necessary to discuss what kind of play they want to make: their decision will affect what they want the outcome of the operation to be. Also, they need to decide what kind of an accident it was and who was to blame. Again, this might affect their attitude towards the boy's death, recovery or partial recovery.

A vote was taken in which the majority voted for 'vegetable'. A name for the son was chosen: Jerry.

It is interesting to note at what point 'past history' is needed. The process of clarifying 'facts' as they are needed is very much part of this approach. The next exercise extends the past history but uses a method that is, in itself, artistic.

I invited members of the class to lie on the floor in spaces of their own. I explained that I too would lie down once I had finished the explanation. 'We shall build a collage of 'Jerry's life by speaking 'into the air' any lines of dialogue that belong to the people in his life. We do not have to keep to a chronological order; something said when he was a baby can be mixed up with something said in the future.' After an uncertain start the dialogue began to flow, sometimes with slight overlapping when two people spoke at once. (This does not matter.) I occasionally took a turn. We then held a discussion about the information we had gleaned about Jerry.

Step 6

We formed groups of three (two parents and Jerry). 'We are going to look at Jerry before the accident ... What occasion would you like it to be? ... We shall find out what relationships were like between these three people *before* it happened.' The class chose 'buying the car'. They moved into playing out this episode simultaneously, without showing.

This was the first opportunity with this class for 'free' dramatic playing, but, of course, it was far from 'free'. In this case I got class consensus on what the occasion should be – the groups were all to dramatise the same 'car-buying' context. Too much time might be wasted in some groups if the teacher simply leaves pupils to choose their own context. Notice that they should not be encouraged to *show* the work, for the teacher does not want the group to think in terms of what will 'look well when we perform', but rather to let themselves have the experience and *discover* what attitudes emerge.

Notice also that I had made a logistics decision: 'From now on in the lesson there are to be several separate families, each with a "Jerry", with the possibility of moving in quite different directions'. They may discover quite different attitudes, for instance. This, of course, makes for richer comparisons, especially when it comes to the family's reaction to the outcome of the operation.

Step 7

Separating each 'Jerry' from his family group, I then asked this central figure to take up an image of 'Jerry, a victim', someone who is cut off. Each family watched this still image grow, symbolising what the accident had done to him. This is the image they were to perceive when visiting him in hospital.

'Turning your back on your "son", carry out some simple, everyday task at home; a task that you share. But because your mind is on the image you have just seen, you will do the task almost in silence, your thoughts back at the hospital.'

This is a classic example of constraint in dramatic playing mode. (Illustrative/performance would be quite inappropriate.) In not requiring the participants to show emotion, paradoxically, very strong emotion may be felt. Depending on the ability of the group, the teacher could physically place Jerry between the parents, as a symbol of what is on their minds. If they are not likely to cope with this then, as I did, the teacher can place Jerry behind them.

Notice that, although we had moved into dramatic playing, it was not with the *injured* Jerry. Such an interaction is quite a test, and Jerry's attempts to look strange may be more hilarious than the 'parents' can cope with. Hence the exercise in Step 8 might prove to be a protective starting point.

Step 8

Half of the class played Jerry, the rest played a member of the family visiting hospital. (Some of the class had to switch temporarily to being the extra 'Jerrys'.) 'Jerry is sitting on a chair and is having difficulty tying his shoelace. The visitor will try to teach him.' Here we held a discussion about how you 'help' someone while training them towards *in*dependence. When the exercise was over each 'Jerry' was asked to evaluate how successful a 'teacher' his visitor had been and to share his evaluation with the rest of the class.

There are many important features in this exercise. It is not simply chance that it involves shoelaces. An action must be selected that removes the possibility of eye contact between the two actors, for the 'Jerry' character may be too morbid or peculiar to cope with without laughing oneself 'out of role'! By concentrating on *shoes*, the actors can give themselves time to test the degree of embarrassment. This is a classic example of a 'projected' activity, that is one in which the participants' attention is on something *outside* themselves. This allows the avoidance of eye contact and at the same time focuses attention, not on how well the actor is portraying Jerry but on the degree of dependence/independence the experience exploits.

We were now near the end of the session, so we wound up with each family creating two family photographs – before and after the accident.

The work could now continue in a number of directions, but probably the theme already begun, that of dependence/independence in a handicapped person, would be the most fruitful.

Joseph and his Brethren
(with ten/eleven-year olds)

This is a description of a lesson on the bible story. The part that appealed to the pupils most was where Joseph gets pushed into a pit by his brothers. It is an interesting phenomenon of drama that those physical events that are so dramatic in 'real life' can be devastatingly disappointing when dramatised. 'House on fire', 'cliff-edges', 'volcanoes', 'mine disasters' and 'drowning' often turn out to be but a brief laugh, especially those 'dramatic' incidents that are necessarily over in a few seconds, like pushing someone into a pit! Dramatically these can be a terrible let down. As I suggested in Chapter 1 (p. 1), although drama relies partially on mimesis, this is not the whole picture. The dramatisation of pushing Joseph over a cliff must somehow look at the *implication* of that act, otherwise the experience will be a cheap and unsatisfying simulation. Yet there is no doubt that, in the children's minds, this is the central feature of the story. Therefore I devised a way of making it central to the drama, but took a long time getting there *directly* and, once there, the class was involved in some hard thinking and planning. The class knew the story, so the drama was both a recapitulation and a chance to deepen their understanding of it.

Step 1

I began, 'Form pairs. In each pair, one of you is Joseph and the other an Egyptian interviewer. It is many years after the 'pit' incident. Joseph has become a very important adviser to the Pharaoh, and his family are all living in Egypt. The interviewer has heard a rumour that, at one time when Joseph was a boy, all was not well in the family – something about attempted murder. Can you, interviewer, find a clever way of getting Joseph to tell you what happened in his distant past? He may not remember; he may not *want* to remember. Joseph, as you are interviewed, you may find out just how much of the truth you are prepared to recall.'.

One of the paradoxes of drama is that this double distancing, both in time and in opportunity to distort the truth, brings the story and its central feature relating to the 'pit' to the forefront of the participants' minds.

Step 2

I gave the class the chance to share with everyone the extent to which the truth was distorted in a number of pairs. Then I moved to discussing how the brothers felt about the incident after all these years. 'Reverse roles, but this time Joseph is replaced by the elder brother who actually did the pushing. I wonder what he will choose to remember! ...'

When the exercise is over you can take the opportunity to discuss, generally, those kinds of occasion in our own lives when we choose not to remember something we have done.

'We are going back in time now to when Joseph was a child, and we are going to think about how his older brothers hated him: "Yes ... that wretched multicoloured coat ... and his stupid dreams, making *us* bow down to him as though he were the Sun and us the Moons ...".'

Notice this unusual way of *endowing* both the pupils and the teacher with the role of the brothers. The teacher's explanation starts as a proper teacher-explanation: 'We are going back in time now ...,' but gradually the tone (of language style *and* quality of voice) changes to 'stupid dreams' and 'making *us*', etc., clearly indicating whose eyes they are now going to see Joseph through.

Step 3

I then set up a pairs exercise in three very brief phases:

One of each pair was the boy Joseph, the other was an elder brother. 'For this first practice stand side by side, each hammering a stake into the ground. These will be used as part of a sheep-pen.' I discussed the length of the stake and the differences of strength of a man and a boy. 'Do not interact; simply show the differences between the mannish and boyish ways of knocking in a stake – pure miming.'

'Now, "out of role" for the next step. Be *any* two brothers. The elder is going to *teach* the younger how to knock in a stake. What kind of thing will the older one feel he has to draw his brother's attention to?'

'Now you will be "in role" again as young Joseph and the elder brother. The brother is determined to teach this lad how to drive in a stake. Joseph, however, is equally determined to use this as an opportunity to tell his brother about one of his wonderful dreams, in which all his elder brothers bowed down to him! ... See who wins!'

This is a 'classic' improvisational structure in which each character is the other's constraint!

Step 4

At this point the class had some taste of the resentment felt by the elder brothers, enough for them to begin to tackle 'pushing down the pit'. One way of doing this, which I chose, is along the following line: 'Let's break off; I want a word before Joseph arrives ... He'll be here with the grub in a while, if he's got the strength to carry it, that is ...'.

It is possible to come 'out of role' at this point, just to check that the class has picked up who and where they are in the story.

'There's a pit over there ...' I used my role to drop in the idea of *murder without spilling blood*! Then it became necessary to turn it into a problem-solving exercise. 'It won't be our fault if he "falls" over the edge ... got too near ... (notice the deliberate use of colloquial language) ... Trouble is, how do we persuade him to go over there to the pit ... and near enough ... to the edge ... for us to ...!'

I hoped at this point that the class, since they knew the story, would also think of another problem – The rich coat he wears is never off his back! (If that was not forthcoming, I would lead into it.) 'What about father ... What will we say to him? ... take the coat back with animal's blood on? ... but how do we persuade him to take it off?'

I then had the choice of organising the following, 'in' or 'out of role' (it is easier '*out* of role'): 'In small groups, each of you pick a Joseph, a *temporary* Joseph. Here we shall try out what will or won't work.'

This device of holding the equivalent of a rehearsal *within* the dramatic playing experience can occasionally be very useful. It is an example of using an illustrative/performance device, that is trying out an idea for others to view *within* their dramatic playing. It also allows for experiment, revision, reflection and assessment. Notice that the most satisfactory solution, as agreed by the class, will be the one used when it comes to 'the real thing'.

I circulated the groups, making sure they understood that they had to be subtle enough not to rouse Joseph's suspicions. I warned the class at this stage that, when it comes to the 'real thing', I would play Joseph: '... and he get's suspicious mighty easily!'. Each group in turn then demonstrated its solution.

This use of the descriptive mode, in order to offer a solution to something (it occurs later in the 'Zoo' lesson (p. 97)), can be very effective, producing thoughtful work.

Once a method of tricking Joseph had been selected, using one group's or a mixture of groups' ideas, the scene was set for Joseph to arrive. I checked that the 'pit' area had been defined. Then, 'as if from afar' (that is hands cupped as though calling a long distance): 'Brothers, I've got the sack of food. Can you give me a hand? ... it's heavy ...'. And so the scene began. *But* I had warned them, 'out of role', that the moment they aroused Joseph's suspicions the drama would be over, for we know that in the story the brothers succeeded in their plan.

Much depends on the maturity of the class. Some may find it quite difficult *collectively* to take full responsibility – children rarely have to do so in their own lives. This is something they can learn, and drama provides the opportunity. The teacher should judge the extent to which they are capable of applying themselves harder in this respect. If the teacher demands too much, then frustration will lead to loss of interest. On the other hand, a sufficient degree of frustration is a powerful stimulus for learning, and will lead to a feeling of satisfaction at 'having won in the end'.

Step 5

The 'climax' now approached as I used my 'Joseph' role to adjust to the needs of the class. When I, as Joseph, finally allowed myself to both remove my coat and go to the edge of the pit, I prepared to move into a totally different drama form from the dramatic playing in which we were then engaged. One class I did this with ingeniously wrung their hands in despair over a supposed lamb that had accidentally fallen down the pit. None of the adult brothers were small enough to get down but, of course, 'Dear little Joseph', was, 'the right size ... and hadn't you better take your beautiful coat off so that it doesn't get dirty ...?'.

One of the key differences between the two activities of dramatic playing and illustrating/performance is that the first works more imaginatively at a *mental* level, whereas the second is more dependent on things 'looking right.' Notice here that the curious convention of the child actors playing adults and the adult playing a child, *and* of *size* being a critical feature within the plot, is found acceptable to everyone *because the belief is 'in their head'*.

I allowed myself to be pushed, but went down in slow motion, finishing up on my back on the floor. As I began to 'descend' I *narrated*, thus turning the experience into a storytelling with descriptive actions: 'And they watched their brother ...' (narrated from *their* perspective, not Joseph's) '... disappear into the blackness of the pit ... until they could hardly see him at all ... *and then* ... when they realised what they had done, they move backwards, as one body, from the edge of the pit ... ' (now the narrating has turned to explicit *instructing*) '... they turned round, picked up their gear and, with one of them carrying the boy's coat, they walked in the direction of home, knowing that they had to find a way to tell their father that his favourite son was dead.'.

The mood is right for reflection, perhaps talking about the sequence, writing the story and preparing to tell it to the School Assembly. Any presentation should not only involve the bare story, but also describe what they have understood of what it meant to the brothers, for this has been the 'learning area'. Alternatively they could create a collage for the classroom wall. They should now know what the teacher means who ponders, 'I wonder how we can show the jealousy and the guilt in a collage?'.

The Silver Sword
(with twelve/thirteen-year olds)

This work with young adolescents was based on Serraillier's novel, *The Silver Sword* (1960) (which they had been studying as part of their English Literature course) about the effect of World War II on Polish refugees. A father named Joseph is searching for the young children who disappeared while he was imprisoned by the Nazis. Having escaped he searches among the rubble of a ruined Warsaw and finds a 'world-wise' nine-year old called Jan. Joseph gives up hope of finding his family and plans to set off for the safety of Switzerland. He gives Jan a family heirloom of a silver sword and asks him to promise that, should he ever come across his two daughters and son, they should be told where their father has gone and follow. Joseph intends making his getaway from Warsaw by jumping on a goods train at a certain spot where Jan knows it slows down. The text continues: 'As they sat there waiting, Joseph said, "I have much to thank you for, and I don't even know your name.".'.

This forms the beginning of a 12-line excerpt of conversation between the two characters which we used in this sequence. It provided an excellent opportunity both to make a close study of the text and to write and perform creatively. That section of the book is written entirely from Joseph's point of view, giving only *his* thoughts and feelings. First I asked the students, in small groups, to devise a performance of the text. They were instructed to use the two characters, plus a narrator who would supply Joseph's thoughts, as given to us by the author. A second narrator was used for the neutral description of the action.

When they had shown their performances at the end of the first lesson, I warned them that we were going to work differently on the same text for the second lesson. This time they were to angle the performance from *Jan's* point of view, while *keeping to the same dialogue*. They were to rewrite all of the private thoughts supplied by the author, and invent Jan's private thoughts, to be performed by the narrator. When one group suggested to me that the 'neutral facts' might become distorted in Jan's memory of the occasion, I agreed that, if they wished, these could be changed as well. The rewriting took the whole lesson (something like an hour – it seemed to grip their imagination), so we did not see their performances until the third lesson.

We wound the work up by looking at other sections of the novel and noting which character's eyes the author uses at different points in the story.

Skin Deep

(with fourteen/fifteen-year olds)

Skin Deep is a play by Paul Swift (unpublished) about racism and pubertal sexual awareness. It is set mainly in South Africa. One of the problems that besets the study of a play-text by a Drama or English class is that there is usually so much of it! Ploughing through a play, scene by scene, can kill it. Yet sound recordings may not be available, so what is the alternative? One solution is to introduce a dramatic activity that is so arresting as a prelude to the play that the pupils *want* to read the whole play. This happened with my work on Miller's *The Crucible*.

Another method involves devising a 'collage' that includes the teacher's choice of a particular thread through the play, a careful selection of very short relevant excerpts, small groups' being responsible for casting and rehearsing the excerpts, and a final 'showing' of the whole collage with teacher-narration piecing the scenes together.

For *Skin Deep* I chose, with the class, to work on the theme of the 'liberal' mother's changing attitude to blacks. Each small group had copies of the full text. I also handed out the line references for the script plus the narration I would be giving. With this information they could, at least crudely, piece together where their particular scene stood in relation to the plot and to the development of the racism theme. I cannot include the whole text here, but below is the information I handed out which gives some idea of the approach.

****

Skin Deep by Paul Swift

The narration is from the angle of Mrs Vera Cassidy.

VERA: It's the story of two people. (p. 1) . . . to . . .
VERA: The black man'll come and get you! (p. 2)

This is the story of two families. One is a white family – Vera, her husband Mike and their son Elvis – who are persuaded to move from the pit unemployment of the North-east of England to Johannesburg, where Mike can get a job in a gold-mine some 30 miles away from where they live. The other is a South African black family who, because they have lost their right to live in Soweto (near Johannesburg), leave their young son Shaka behind to finish his education. His elder sister Lonkuleko (Joy) stays to try to keep an eye on Shaka. However, with her job as a 'kitchen girl' in Johannesburg, her half-day off per week means that brother and sister are virtually separated. She has little idea of how involved he is becoming in the political protests against schooling.

JOY: I spent the next two days . . . (p. 18) . . . to . . .
VERA: So maybe, you and me can be friends, eh? (p. 19)

Meanwhile, Vera's husband, Mike, is having to learn quickly about fitting into 'white' society. He has inadvertently caused a spot of bother at work and is being moved, temporarily, to a gold-mine much further away from home.

MIKE: I'll be home once a month pet. (p. 23) . . . to . . .
VERA: . . . 'cos I don't bloody like them! (p. 23)

It is Joy's seventeenth birthday and Vera gives her permission to have the day off to visit her brother in Soweto. It happens to be 16 June, 1976, the day of an uprising by the school population. She cannot find Shaka and, because of the disruption to transport, she has difficulty getting back to Vera's house.

JOY: It was very late, the next day . . . (p. 27) . . . to . . .
VERA: I'm not sure Elvis, but I think you've shot her brother. (p. 28)

Vera attempts to take Shaka, who has been wounded in the leg, to the nearby hospital where she is working as a part-time nurse, but several hours later ...

VERA: I've never been so disgusted in my life. (p. 31) ... to ...
VERA: Come on, let's get him into the house. (p. 31)

It is during Shaka' recuperation that the relationship between Elvis and Joy undergoes a radical change, from hostility to affection. Elvis hates his Afrikaans school, and it is during his long periods of playing truant, when his mother is at work, that the two young people develop a fondness for each other. This has now reached a point where, most nights, Elvis creeps into Joy's bed, a relationship which at that time in South Africa was considered illegal. Shaka senses that something is going on and, even though he grows to rely on Vera, he can hardly mask his hatred of the young 'white master'.

One night the police break into Joy's bedroom – just one of their routine 'sweeps' into the bedrooms of black employees. Fortunately, Elvis had not arrived – Shaka, Elvis and Joy had just had words, a barely concealed row – but in her sleepiness, Joy says, 'You're late. I didn't expect you tonight.'. The police seize on this giveaway, and Joy quickly invents some black boy she was expecting, a fictitious 'Gideon'.

CAPTAIN: You know what sergeant? (p. 40) ... to ...
JOY: I swear to God, Mrs. Cassidy, I've never had a black boy here. (p. 42)

Several weeks later, the day when Shaka is about to make a secret flight over the border, he reports to Vera that Joy has been having fainting fits and sickness.

VERA: Go up to the house and put the kettle on, Shaka, there's a good lad. (p. 45) ... to ...
SHAKA: I'm the black man who's coming to get you! (p. 46)

****

It is important that the 'showing' is formalised, to the extent that each group occupies a given space, for example to form part of a semicircle of separate scenes. Each group should be alert to the need to move smoothly into action in response to the narration, so that the exercise has a feeling of being a presentation. In this way the play is seen as a coherent whole. It also stimulates the pupils to find out about the 'missing bits'.

The Zoo
(with nine/ten-year olds)

'Let's do a drama about wild animals escaping from a zoo' was the suggestion voted for by the class.

Step 1

I began with the children in a circle of chairs. I addressed them in role: 'I know you are busy people ... the zoo management appreciates your coming at such short notice ... but you will appreciate that, after what's happened this week, the matter is urgent ... the council will just close us down if we cannot guarantee the safety of the public ... The old lady, mercifully, has recovered consciousness, but she was badly mauled ... How the lion escaped we're not sure yet ... but it seems the compound was not sufficiently secure ... The council says we have to make all animal cages and compounds *escape proof* ... Now this is where you come in ... I understand you have all had experience designing animal accommodation ... specialising with different kinds of animals, I'm told ... Which of you has designed for monkeys? ... bears? ... lions? ...'.

Step 2

After this they were asked to go into groups, according to their choice of animal, and to start designing. During the week following this Drama lesson their class teacher gave them further time and advice, so when they returned for the second lesson they arrived with impressively detailed and clearly laid out designs on large sheets of paper. I had six fairly large tables in the classroom we were working in, so I asked each group to lay out their design on a table top. We Sellotaped them down.

Step 3

I asked the six groups to 'swap round' so that each was standing round another group's design. I then set them the task of examining the design in front of them and familiarising themselves with its security measures. If anything was unclear, they could informally invite someone over from the group that was responsible for that particular design for further explanation.

Step 4

When they were satisfied that they understood the security intention of the design in front of them, they were instructed to try to find a possible flaw in the design. 'Yes, I know this is ruthless, but in matters of security we have to risk hurting people's feelings ... Keeping the zoo open is more important than suffering the indignity of having your design criticised ...'. If they found a flaw, instead of *explaining* it to the rest of us they were to *show* some incident that could hypothetically occur as a result of this weak security.

Step 5

Of course, they had no difficulty in finding 'flaws'! As it turned out, not surprisingly, their scenes demonstrated *human* frailty rather than faults in the design. As one group showed us, an animal escaped because the keeper felt too tired after a late night to check the lock on the second gate. Thus this step consisted of group rehearsals of their demonstrations. I went round challenging them on the clarity of their communication.

Step 6

Each group demonstrated their ideas in turn. (Note this use of illustrative/performance activity with nine-year old children *within* their role as designers.) After each performance the 'audience' (the rest of the class) was invited to ask questions. Of course, the members of the group who had originally carried out the design in question were vociferous in their challenge of what they sometimes saw as a distorted version of their work.

Step 7

A final discussion which just *flowed* from the scenes, and which I eventually steered towards more general issues, related to 'the human factor' in matters of safety. These lessons occurred at the time of Chernobyl, so many topical links were made.

The above sequence has qualities that appear to match Dorothy Heathcote's M of E approach: the pupils were 'in role' as experts; their thinking was demonstrated through records (the designs); and they learnt something about the topic in hand. However, as we shall see from the rest of this chapter in which I describe two of Dorothy's lessons, this exercise is but a pale imitation of M of E proper.

The following is an account of two themes taught by Dorothy Heathcote using the M of E approach. These are not detailed, but I hope there is enough to give the flavour of the work.

Heroes
(with six/seven-year olds)

The American class Dorothy met were full of 'Batman'; they arrived wearing 'Batman' shirts and even offered *her* one to wear! She was to work with them in drama over a four-week period and, not surprisingly, she sought to broaden their fantasy hero into something worth pursuing for that length of time. For this reason she chose 'heroes' as the theme, but she did not tell them this.

She started by carrying a lettuce (a choice of object which may surprise English readers, but this teaching took place in America where lettuce is a daily food), examining it carefully. From that starting image she slowly established that they were people who ran a 'lettuce warehouse and laboratory'. First she got them all talking 'lettuce' responsibilities and doing 'lettuce actions', in other words establishing their collective responsibility for nurturing, protecting from pests, selling, packaging and distributing lettuces, as though they had been a joint-working enterprise for years. Then she dropped in the stimulus that would give the experience its dynamic for the rest of the four weeks.

Looking through her mail (in her role as the 'lettuce laboratory' manager, of course) she came across a letter from the President of America, marked PRIVATE AND CONFIDENTIAL: STATE SECRETS.

The envelope was oversize and bore words like FROM THE OFFICE OF THE PRESIDENT, THE WHITE HOUSE, which the children could read (those that could read – this is something Dorothy had to find out) as she opened it. She read out the letter. In it, the President suggested that America did not have enough heroes and, having heard how good an organisation they were (how efficient, how imaginative and how good at keeping plans secret), he wondered whether they would consider applying their expertise to creating new heroes. Such a venture would require them to leave their present premises secretly and find an alternative site for their confidential work, . . . etc.

One way of beginning to find out about their reading and linguistic ability was for Dorothy to stumble over one or two words as though she was not sure of them. This gave the children a chance to look over her shoulder or guess at what the words might be. She could allow herself to be put off by the formality of the language so that she appeared unsure of what the letter might mean.

The six/seven-year olds readily agreed to take on the President's challenge and had to decide where in America they should go in order to have a 'secret place'. She had already prepared a large, hand-drawn map of the USA. This was marked only with 'America's secret Places', like the 'badlands' of the Dakotas, the Grand Canyon of Arizona and the Mauna Loa crater of Hawaii. After a lot of map-gazing and some discussion of where *they* lived in relation to all these strange places, they chose to move to the 'other side of Lake Erie', which was thought to have secret places and wasn't too far!

The next stage of the work involved deciding how to vacate their present building without drawing attention to what they were doing. Thus loading a truck with lettuces, etc. (having taken an inventory – dictated to Dorothy and written up on big sheets – of all their laboratory contents first) and moving out in the dark became a major hurdle. It was at about this point that Dorothy warned them that she was going to test them, by asking the kind of questions a traffic warden might ask about where they were going and why. (This *demonstrating* a role rather than *being* it is a key feature of M of E, and indeed of most uses of T in R.) The 'test', of course, is to do with not giving away the President's secret.

Having 'proved' themselves by their clever answers, the pupils responded positively when Dorothy asked them if they could cope with another crisis – this time the engine of their vehicle would not start. So up went the bonnet and the six/seven-year olds had to explain to the 'know-nothing-about-the-inside-of-trucks Dorothy' what the different parts were called and how they functioned. Gradually she led up to a theatrical moment when, at their bidding, 'Eureka!', the engine came back to life. But there was more to it than that. She continued the notion of 'prying eyes' (initiated by the night-time removal, and continued by the traffic warden) and occasionally role-played a 'watcher', establishing that, if they were so busy with their engine problem, they wouldn't be free to have to answer any embarrassing questions. She alternated the 'watcher' role with her 'real' one of being with them and worrying about *that* 'watcher', thereby increasing the tension in two ways. There is always the danger with this age group that they will solve any problem in seconds, but the paradoxical dramatic constraint here is that it pays them *not* to start the engine too soon!

Dorothy saying, 'Can you cope with another crisis?', preceded a further problem – a puncture!

Notice this teacher-style of putting it to the class that they have a choice of coping with another problem, rather than just springing one on them. This not only establishes the possibility of controlling what they want to happen in the drama but, more importantly, focuses on *their coping* rather than on the arbitrariness of the problem. Rather than being the victims of a problem, they are *spectators* able to watch and assess themselves as they respond to it.

On the surface the puncture looks like a repetition of the first problem. In fact it was, in practice, subtly different, for this time Dorothy did not play the 'watcher'. Here the satisfactions were to be drawn from the task itself for if the children were to be *experts* at creating heroes for America, then before they moved into that major work they had to have a series of experiences that would help them *believe in* their own collective ability. This is more than an individual child's cleverness; this is to do with 'ensemble' responsibility – collective *characterisation* as I called it in Chapter 3 (p. 50).

If the members of a class have difficulty in working together (as I understand was the case with this class), or working on the chosen theme (after all, 'lettuces' seems a long way from 'Batman!), then it is important that both they and the teacher find out what they are like on a *preliminary* joint task – a *foretaste* – before the major work begins. But achievement is not a matter of the slick miming of changing a wheel – *that doesn't achieve anything*, apart from moving the 'plot' on. A feeling of success can only be gained as a result of hard work, related to the physics, mathematics and engineering of changing a wheel. The children should be pressed by the teacher into thinking harder than they thought themselves capable. This will involve drawing their own diagrams (in this instance, with sticks on the sandy edge of the road), following the teacher's blackboard work, labelling parts, looking at pictures in truck handbooks, the give-and-take of ideas and trying things out in *carefully monitored* miming. When the spare wheel is finally on, they know they have 'grown' a little.

It is worth noting here that, when I originally typed out this section, I submitted it to Dorothy to check that I had given the correct information about her lessons. I had written in the above paragraph, '... looking at pictures in *car* handbooks ...'. She returned it to me with 'car' crossed out, adding, '*Truck* handbook was our reference, not just any car book. Experts don't use any old materials.'! This comment says something about the craft of the M of E approach, and perhaps also explains why I am so bad at it!

The class then switched from the map of America to road-maps, in order to work out its itinerary. It was during this work that Dorothy imperceptibly moved into the 'hero' theme, in an unexpected way that had the potential for a radical change in the quality of the drama. Dorothy used another teacher in a secondary role – secondary in the sense of it being supportive to the work. The teacher, dressed in a green drape, carried a pristinely white tablecloth shaped and held like a baby (but clearly *not* a baby). She also carried a long pole with a cardboard, spear-like end, and attached to it the suggestion of a star. Dorothy prefers to term such a role as a 'full role', as the individual is locked into his/her role by the paraphernalia of clothes, baby and pole.

At first the second teacher (following Dorothy's instructions) just stood in their midst and was ignored by the class, who 'got on' with what they were doing. It is important to appreciate that the seeds of this 'being watched' experience had already been planted by Dorothy in the earlier 'engine not working' problem. (Here Dorothy worked like a dramatist, providing an indication early in the 'play' of something that was to grow in importance at a later stage.) So initially the children saw this being watched as an extension of what they had been through before, but this 'watcher' did not go away.

Gradually, individual children pointed out the presence of the standing figure to Dorothy. When attention started to focus on the woman she spoke, saying something like, 'His daddy and me have heard you are going to make heroes ... my baby ...'.

And so there was a *partial* unfolding of an opportunity which the children may or may not have wanted to take up. It was at this point that Dorothy employed the classic use of T in R: as someone sceptical about any kind of distraction and having an unwillingness to understand the children's interpretation of what the woman was trying to say. It is worth noting here that many teachers would fall into the trap of doing the opposite, that is seizing upon evidence of any child's grasp of the woman's meaning and pushing forward enthusiastically. In fact it was the *lack* of support, even hindrance, from Dorothy's role that, paradoxically, invited the children to challenge her. It also required them to clarify to themselves what *they* thought the newcomer meant, so that they could get their teacher to understand that she was missing something important. The more Dorothy, in role, said, 'Let's get on ...' (her tone of voice and doubtful glances in the direction of the woman betraying fear!), the more they clung to what the intruder was requesting, *and* the more they believed in the baby, as they proceeded to explain to Dorothy that they could bring the baby up to become a hero.

I have already illustrated examples of the use of real and non-real objects. In Chapter 2 (p. 13) I discussed the use of a real, pictorial or mimed telephone; in this chapter (in the Nativity and 'Vegetable' examples, pp. 81 & 83) an empty chair was used to represent a person; also in this chapter (in the Nativity, p. 81) the blue scarf initially stood for the 'Virgin Mary' and later became the baby we 'christened'. In the Heroes example a green drape represented a baby. It was very important that neither Dorothy nor the teacher with the drape used overt 'baby-type' actions with the material. It was the children who had to acquire 'ownership' of the baby. If they didn't want to own it then Dorothy would have to try to pick up what they did want. 'That's not a baby', said one child dismissively to the 'mother'. 'No, it's a table-cloth baby', was the neutral-voiced response from Dorothy! Such a reply neatly disposes of the unnecessary delusion that in drama we are supposed to represent a world out there with accuracy. The power of drama, particularly of the M of E approach, lies in the fact that we all know it's a table-cloth and are not pretending otherwise. This releases us to *use* the object as a 'stand in'. Of course, in this instance the baby became firmly present. This was illustrated by the fact that, when Dorothy at a later stage, testing their acceptance, muttered something like, 'That baby needs a face ...', the protesting reply was, 'He's got a face!'.

So the notion of bringing up a baby to be heroic crept in and gradually took over the rest of the work, which included making a long list of what it means to be heroic ('not telling on anyone', for example). Then the work took off in the direction of their having to provide model behaviour themselves for the baby to copy. This line was introduced by Dorothy; she saw it as having potential in their understanding of heroes and she took advantage of her influence as the teacher to impose it. *But* she was at the same time alert to *how* they were responding to the idea. If they were not engaged she would then change tack. Some teachers are afraid to impose in this way, even though they can recognise potential learning, yet sometimes this is where their responsibility should lie. Of course, the problem for inexperienced teachers may be that they do not trust themselves to know how to retrieve a failing situation should the class not be interested in their idea. In this case the children did take up the 'exemplary behaviour in front of the baby' idea.

All sorts of rules about the children's own behaviour had to evolve, with checks and punishments. Gradually they focused on 'eating' behaviour. So with only imaginary meal-tables laid with depicted (that is, drawn on sheets of paper) dishes and trays of food, including a bottle of milk for the baby, they had to set examples of table behaviour, miming the eating and drinking with accurate gesture. Notice how the *baby* had become the silent watcher. The emphasis throughout this work was on the pupils looking at and evaluating their own behaviour. They were for most of the time in the dramatic playing mode, but this was heightened by activating the 'spectator' in themselves. They were not 'performing', while wondering how some spectator in an audience 'out there' would appreciate what they were doing. The spectator is both inside the dramatic playing, 'the watcher', the 'mother' or the 'baby', *and* 'in the head'.

Naming the baby became important. Someone suggested the 'Great Sun' as a name for someone who was to become a hero, but this was thought to be premature – a name for an *established* hero rather than a hero in the making. So 'Moonlight' was substituted. They worked out an elaborate ritual. This involved them all being in a boat in the middle of the lake, with the moonlight catching the baby's hair as they named him.

Various examples of heroic behaviour were enacted for everyone to watch. (Notice here that the six/seven-year olds were moving into the descriptive mode, because the logic required it.) Towards the end of the work Dorothy dropped in, 'Do we need the baby in our eyes any more?'. The green drape ceased to be used as a 'stand in' for the physical presence of the baby. Instead it became a symbol of a different kind: a parchment for recording their thoughts about heroic behaviour, that is ordinary, everyday behaviour made to seem important. The table-cloth was spread out, they all sat round it and the teacher wrote directly onto the cloth whatever they dictated to her. It became a 'Creed for Heroes'.

The Restaurant
(with eight to ten-year olds)

This exercise involved a group of seemingly unmotivated American children. Dorothy was asked by their teacher to focus on Maths.

'If we were going to run the best restaurant in town, how many things on our menu could we sell for a dollar?', was Dorothy's opening gambit. Notice the 'If we *were* . . . how many things *could* . . .'. Dorothy felt she could not trust taking them into the *present* at this point. Even as she spoke she was wondering how to take this step. As they called out ideas she made a haphazard list on the blackboard – some items drawn, some written boldly and confidently, some hesitant according to the degree of interest she 'heard' in their suggestions, and, of course, showing immediate acceptance and respect for what they offered.

Her next step was to start a discussion of the items on the list, asking a few questions and making a few comments. But as she did so she began rewriting items from the list on a big clear section of the blackboard. This time it became clear that this new list had some order to it, both in content and form. It became a menu, but *no longer a menu on a blackboard* for she was beginning to treat the blackboard as a big window. She began 'cleaning' it. It was *the restaurant* window, with its menu painted on it, and as she 'cleaned' it she was saying things like, 'I've noticed most restaurants have some kind of "sign" . . . so that you recognise it quickly . . . Shall we have a sign? . . . What do you think?'. (Notice this, 'shall *we* have a sign?'. 'We-ness' was being established.) A logo of a 'chef's hat was suggested. 'I don't know whether I can draw a chef's hat . . . Whereabouts do you think it ought to go? . . . Here? . . . Oh, here! . . . Tell me if I'm doing it right . . .', and so on. Through the *window* the restaurant was established, *and they were all there in front of it*. They were in the *here* and it was then a relatively easy matter to move into the *now* of the action.

Dorothy continued to mention 'cleanliness' as 'one of the things we are noted for in our restaurant', and invited them to clean other windows. (Notice that one of the features of this action was that the teacher was involved in a task that, for the most part, took her eyes *away from* the class, signalling another kind of trust.) They then, through concensus, arrived at a name for 'our' restaurant. Because their class teacher wanted a 'maths' bias to the work, Dorothy's next point of reference was to do with money and security: 'Where do we put our takings . . . overnight?'. (She gave a hint of a vulnerablility in the place.) The class suggested hiding them. This moved the drama into a new phase, ostensibly about the problem of where to hide the cash, but was used by Dorothy to establish 'ownership' of the restaurant and its different departments: 'The pantry, you think . . . Who's in charge of the pantry this week?'. (Notice this deliberate exploitation of temporariness, which is less threatening than permanent commitment.) Thus a 'spatial' sense and a 'responsibility' sense were started. Eventually it was decided that the dollar notes should be hidden among the liver!

Having started with the 'menu' idea, Dorothy intended to take this up again, linking it, as before, with the restaurant prices. The students seemed to be interested in steaks. Taking up this idea, Dorothy determined on the idea of a 'specialist menu' with all kinds of steak refinements, and prices to match. However, the class by then had other ideas. They launched themselves into a restaurant design project. They decided to be a 'steak' eating-place. Its chief feature was to be a massive cylindrical tube like a tree in the middle of the restaurant, into which a whole bullock would be lowered before the eyes of the customers. They would then choose which part of the beast they wanted cooking! The 'ears' were to be the delicacy reserved for privileged guests to take home 'gift-wrapped', of course.

This is a very good example of a class taking over the direction but not, it has to be emphasised, taking over the drama. It would be impossible for an inexperienced class to structure the process – the size and the immaturity of the group would deny them a satisfying experience – but they *could* choose a new route. *It is still the teacher's responsibility to help them 'make their idea happen'.* It is the teacher's superior knowledge of education and theatre that will give the class the experience they want. Many teachers do not understand this and feel that, once a class has an idea, they have to stand back and let its members be 'creative'! This is to misunderstand both creativity and the teacher's job. The teacher does not have to relinquish the (in this case) mathematical bias, but has to look for new opportunities within the new context. The costing of the 'bullock sections' would become an issue, once the students had dealt with the mathematics of their design (that is the size of the cylinder vis-à-vis the restaurant dining area and the size of bullocks!). The *quality, size* and *weight* of the portions would then become relevant. The chances are that, because the cylinder was the children's own idea, they would see the necessity for the accurate, mathematical work, using the correct tools of the 'real' world. The strength of Dorothy's work is that the fiction sustains a respect for the physical world which, of course, is of enormous interest to the Primary School age group, and to teachers who have a curriculum to follow!

With bullocks out of the student's systems (as it were!), Dorothy moved to a different aspect of numeracy. This time she dealt with the quantity of cutlery required and its organisation within the dining-room and kitchen. 'How many knives do we need in use at any one time, especially at our most busy time, to ensure that there is always a clean knife ready?' This is a 'knife-flow' time and number problem. Some children became occupied with this; others, in small groups, moved into designing the menu; others looked at ingredients for the salad bar, to go with the steak; yet others moved on to designing a 'salad mural' (giving attention to estimation and proportion) for the restaurant walls.

It cannot be overstressed that teacher-behaviour is crucial to the success of the work. Almost continually in a role, using the language style of a fellow worker, the teacher encourages, challenges, empowers, muses, asks questions, worries and negotiates. These are the kinds of thing that *teachers* do, but in the M of E approach it is the *role* that can do these things so much more effectively.

6 Aims and Objectives

It may seem strange that a chapter with this title should be found towards the end of a book on drama education. So often such a title is used to introduce a subject, but in this text I felt we could only think about aims in the light of the preceding philosophy and practice. Also, the reader will have become used to my own personal way of describing things, so there will be some familiarity with what follows. For instance I shall continually be referring to content/form, a concept more accessible in the light of earlier chapters.

The history of Drama Education in England (Bolton, 1984) tells a pendulum-swinging story. From the early days of text-centred drama of the Speech and Drama teachers, to the headier days of the child-centred approach of Peter Slade (1954), and from the content-centred work of Dorothy Heathcote, to the skill-centred approach of some current writers, trends often borne of political pressures have pushed teachers in contrary directions.

I think it is useful here to attempt to categorise the aims that have been variously followed by past practitioners. In spite of the wide philosophical divergences, it is possible to detect but four main aims that all drama teachers at all times have tended to maintain. There have been those who:

1 place an emphasis on content;
2 promote drama for personal growth;
3 see drama principally as a means of social development;
4 hold teaching about the dramatic art form as a priority.

In several recent articles (1989, 1990) I attempted to elaborate on these categories. I claimed that the good Drama teacher attempts to move forward on all of these fronts simultaneously, sometimes, because of the nature of the work or the nature of the class, giving more attention to one than the other. When it came to expanding on Category 4 I found myself at odds with some current writers, including those of official DES (1984, 1989, 1990) and NCC (1990) documents. They almost totally ignore dimensions of form which, as shown in earlier chapters, provide the basis for my theory and practice of Drama Education. I am referring to concepts such as focus and tension, which are created by the deliberate manipulation of time and space, and by the imposition of constraints. These critical formal dimensions are given little space in recent literature, almost as though those now writing about drama theory do not really understand the basic nature of drama.

The trap in attempting to categorise lies in the very separation of concepts that should not be isolated. In recent writings I have divided Category 4 into four subcategories:

a Learning how to act;
b Academic learning about drama;
c Learning theatre crafts;
d Learning the basic elements of drama.

But I have been so alienated by the dualism apparent in the *The Arts 5–16* project, in which the writers promote the erroneous notions of Education *through* the Arts and Education *in* the Arts, that I have felt compelled to take Subcategory d from category 4 in order to join it up with Category 1. Hence the concept of 'content/form', which I hope will re-establish in teachers' minds that when you are working in one of the Arts, you are drawing on the interdependence of the two. Category 4, losing its critical 'basic elements' to Category 1, can now be described as 'Theatre knowledge, Techniques and Crafts. Diagramatically, the four categories can be expressed as shown in the next figure.

Learning about content/form

Most writers in the Arts, even those that seek to promote a separation between Education *through* the Arts and Education *in* the Arts, agree that the Arts are concerned with bringing about some new understanding. I quote from the document *The Arts 5–16* (NCC, 1990):

> 'The arts . . . are concerned with many different ways of knowing the world . . .' (p. 26 A Curriculum Framework)

Aims in Drama teaching

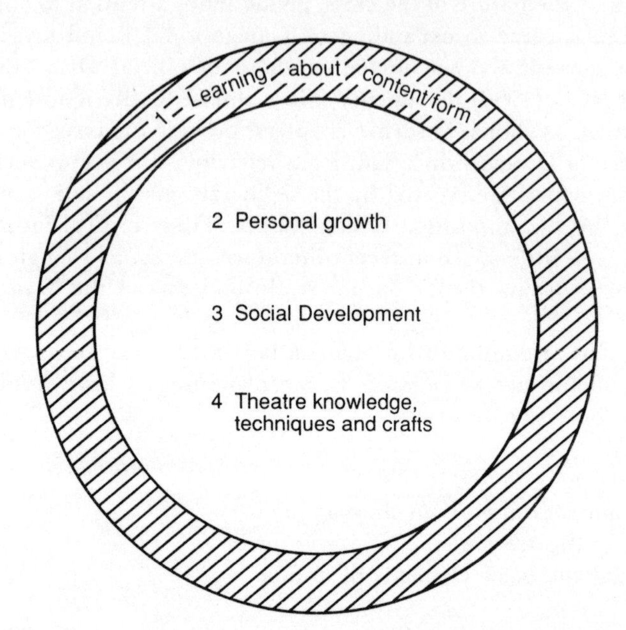

> 'The arts ... are concerned not only with what we perceive in the world but with the *qualities* of human perceptions; with *how* we experience the world.' (*ibid.*)

> 'They may also be creative in the more profound sense of generating new ways of seeing.' (p. 27 A Curriculum Framework)

> '... at some times the artist is an iconoclast who challenges prevailing attitudes and values; at others, artists are 'the voice of the community', shaping images and artifacts to give form to a community's deepest values and convictions.' (*ibid.*)

All of the above quotes give support to the idea that the Arts are to do with understanding the world anew, in respect of the qualities of our perceptions and the values we bring to bear on what we perceive. Drama teachers, perhaps more than other Arts teachers, have tended in the last 20 years or so to articulate the purpose of their work in these kinds of terms. Although such statements may be true of other Art forms – certainly it is apparent in all written forms of Art – it is easier for Drama teachers and playwrights to see their work being aimed at engaging directly with the world, for Drama relies on the world for its material. If you like, 'the world' is the dramatist's *curriculum*. But as I have said in Chapter 3 (p. 36), it is not the playwright's job to describe the world in a *factual* sense, but in a *truthful* sense. The playwright illuminates some kind of truth about the world (which, of course, includes ourselves), and s/he achieves this through the use of *form*. The 'content' of a play is 'content-as-illuminated-by-form', and the emerging truth is born of that content/form particularity. Of course, for the sake of convenience in dealing with it we, as an audience or as academics, may generalise from it. This is a reductionist process which is always in danger of denying the original experience, like contenting ourselves with labelling Shakespeare's *Othello* as being about 'jealousy'. Unavoidably, the moment we attempt to reflect on how an art product might have significance for us, we move away from its particularity. There is an interaction occurring between the particular that is the play and the particular that is *me*, and if, further, I want to share my response with someone else, I will no doubt be driven to finding a sufficient level of generalisation to afford communication.

The interdependence of content/form has implications for the teacher and pupils in the classroom. The world is also *their* curriculum, to be illuminated by dramatic form. In this respect the teacher and students in the classroom are not doing anything different from what playwrights, directors and actors are trying to achieve. To say that it is possible, as *The Arts 5–16* project claims, to use drama as a method of relating to content in some way that is different from the kind of drama one uses in 'making drama' is absurd, for any 'making drama' *must* be about some significant content.

There is a form of dramatic usage in schools, often referred to as Simulation or Role-play for skill training, that has little to do with dramatic art, where children take on roles in order to assimilate facts or develop behavioural skills. Although it may well carry the 'imperative tension' of something important happening, what in fact often happens is that everyone's attention is focused on the skill of the participant: 'Is s/he handling the simulated interview adequately?' . . . 'Is s/he conducting this simulated counselling sensitively?' . . . 'Does s/he (the trainee doctor) answer the patient's (simulated) questions?' . . . 'Does s/he bring the management team to a reasonable point of agreement?' . . . 'Given the alternatives, does s/he arrive at a sensible decision?' . . . 'Does s/he get rattled as we pile on the pressures – in this (of course) fictitious situation?'. Such activities are to drama as diagrams are to visual art – they are denotative rather than connotative. There is no protection either by the fiction (for in this case the supposed fiction replicates the pressures of 'real life' too closely) or by the character; indeed it is one's own personality that is being tested.

Surely the NCC publication, *The Arts 5–16*, cannot be advocating a balanced diet between 'diagrams' and 'paintings', between Simulation and Drama as an art form? I think it more likely that the writers of the project do not understand that *Drama is always about something*. Inescapably, there are always content, theme, substance, subject matter and curriculum. There is no such thing as a division between Education *in* and Education *through* the Arts. Even the simplest form of drama with kindergarten children must be using the art form to illuminate some truth about the world; otherwise dramatic activity simply remains at the 'diagram' level of reiterating facts or practising skills. Let me make it clear that I am not *against* Role-play or Simulation. They have their place in education and training, and, indeed, Drama teachers from time to time may employ such exercises as part of a cumulative sequence. But our overriding aim is always to achieve *understanding* through the art form.

Sometimes you are aware that your work has slipped into something that amounts to no more than Simulation. I have occasionally come across Drama teachers who set up a kind of drama that is little different from a 'discussion'. (I have done it myself in off moments!) I call this kind of work 'Swimming Pool' drama. I have taken the title from those lessons where the teacher poses a problem: 'You are members of the town council. You have one million pounds left over. Do you want to spend it on a swimming pool or a home for the elderly?'. There is little chance of 'ownership' of these roles. There is also little chance of finding an interesting use of, for example, focus or constraint to give the experience form. This is a kind of dramatised discussion, *which may still have educational value but it is not dramatic art*. Here I shall give an example from my own practice of what I mean by dramatic art.

Some time ago I was asked to teach Road Safety to a class of six-year olds. If I had wanted to *avoid* drama I could have set up a simulation exercise, whereby the children had the chance to practise road drill: looking right, left and then right again before crossing an imaginary road. This would amount to Simulation practice – 'drawing diagrams'. But as it was *drama* I wanted to use, I set up a fictitious situation where we invented a five-year old boy called Michael. On his birthday he rushed home from school instead of waiting for his parent and was knocked down by a car. We did *not* simulate the accident. I decided that I should be 'in role' as Michael's parent and the class as Michael's neighbours. What we experienced was the parent arriving home, thinking that Michael must surely have got home first and was hiding: 'Michael? . . . Michael, I know you're hiding . . .', I called, at first in fun and then, as the silence followed each call, more and more desperately. Then I included the neighbours by asking them whether they had seen him – perhaps he was hiding in their homes. Then, on the neighbours' advice, I decided to phone the school, but I was too worried to make the call: 'Could one of you . . .?', and so on. Eventually we learnt there had been an accident and that Michael was in hospital. He had run across a road without looking first.

For me this is working *in* the art form. What we experienced was that moment when a name was called, and there was no answer. The silence was awesome. I believe that it was this silence that took us, the children and me together, close to realising what ignoring the road-safety rules can *amount to*. It also gave some point to learning the Road Safety Code.

To ask of my lesson, 'Was it Education *through* the Arts or Education *in* the Arts?' is totally absurd. As far as I was concerned we were working in the art form using elements of theatre, and we had a firm grasp of the kind of content we were setting out to explore. As a teacher I was observing their understanding of the theme, and whether they could extend the theatrical context I had started: to what extent, for instance, were the children able to enjoy the *withholding* of the news about the accident, so that the tension of not knowing could be fully experienced?; to what extent could they 'pick up' the effectiveness of the counterpoint between the calling and the silence? Notice too the obliqueness of the focus chosen by the teacher to open up this area of knowledge. This is not using drama as a *method*, although the writers of *The Arts 5–16* appear to think it is.

I will give an example from Secondary teaching, again to make my point about choosing material that happened to be in someone's syllabus – this time History. The History textbook included a kind of 'dramatic' activity that was 'diagram drawing' at its worst. The authors, in their chapter on the American War of Independence, included something that looked like a play-script. The rift between the people of New York and the British Government was expressed through the mouths of the owner of a New York coffee house and a well-known customer visiting from London. Each character's dialogue stated the opposing arguments in a way that was meant to help the students remember the relevant viewpoints. This is an example of Simulation, the equivalent of practising Road Safety. The students would no doubt remember the relevant facts as a result of this dramatic technique, *but it is not drama*. I asked my class to become scriptwriters and to turn the text they had in front of them in their History books into 'real' drama. 'How do you speak to your customers when you are setting up a business? . . . Suppose that customer riles you with his erroneous political views? . . .', and the class began to realise the meaning of *subtext*: it is the *constraint* on the owner of the coffee shop that makes drama; it is the things that are *not* said that matter. The paradox of working in the art form of drama in this way is that, like the silence when Michael did not answer (p. 112), we are drawn nearer to the meaning of what is going on because it remains implicit. Again, it becomes nonsense to ask whether we were working *through* the Arts or *in* the Arts.

Form

I hope the above examples also make clear the interdependence of content/form. In Chapters 2 and 3 I drew attention to the basic components of theatre form (not to be confused, as some recent writers are guilty of doing, with theatre conventions or genres). Some of them are listed below as a reminder:

- *Focus* or *Imperative tension* provides the dynamic for dramatic form: our attention is engaged by something that *must* happen;
- *Tension* through the manipulation of time and space;
- *Tension* through the imposition of 'constraints', that is the witholding of true facts, true feelings, true wants;
- *Ritual*;
- *Temporary chaos*, through the *breaking* of constraint or ritual.

There is a cluster of theatrical concepts which form part of tension and ritual: *deception*; *seeming*; *magic*; *order*; *disorder*; *power*; *ambiguity*; *harmony*, *contrast*, etc. Each is part of the excitement of theatre. It is the teacher's responsibility, no matter how young the children are, to foster a sense of theatre which they may or may not be able to articulate. Suppose in the Road Safety lesson above, some of the children were not able to 'withhold' their superior knowledge that Michael had had an accident. I would have had a number of choices: I could have stopped the drama and invited them to 'see what it's like to watch Michael's father calling a child because he does not know what has happened'; when the experience was over I could have talked about whether 'we could have made it more exciting if we had not told Michael's father straightaway'; I could have borne in mind that, the next time I did drama with this class, I would test them with a similar situation where the constraint of withholding the truth for the sake of the drama was again demanded of them. This simple knowledge of the 'game of theatre' is something that Drama classes must understand and appreciate as soon as possible, and teachers should continually be alert to opportunities for teaching that game.

Just as I am critical of the writers of *The Arts 5–16* for encouraging Drama specialists to feel that they can teach their art without respect for content, so I am equally critical of those teachers who give little attention to the need to improve their pupils' ability to handle the art. About two years ago I sat in at a session of a course for teachers from an outer London borough. The tutor asked the class of teachers to write down and classify their aims in teaching Drama. There was a long list dealing with subject matter, and personal and social development, but not one teacher put forward 'improvement in doing drama' as an aim. Indeed, when I suggested that they had missed out his vital aim, there was a slightly shocked response as though I had committed some professional gaffe.

Content

In the theatre and in the classroom, drama is a way into knowledge: it opens up new ways of looking at things. Through theatrical metaphor the world we live in is explored. But while it is possible to *indicate* the door that is being opened by the play or the classroom drama sequence, one cannot specify what any one individual will learn, or even guarantee that s/he will go through that door! Just as one cannot in any absolute sense explain what an art product is about other than in terms of itself, so one cannot identify what a particular person will learn. We can only *indicate* what something is about and *indicate* what we think someone has learnt.

The teacher may be able to plan in broad terms using the notion of learning *area*, but because it is art the teacher is not in a position to be more explicit. I like the concept of 'opening a door'. The Maths teacher, or even the History teacher (the kind who goes for facts, that is), may find it easy to be specific. Indeed, much Simulation-type dramatic method will allow for explicitness. In the Road Safety example above, no doubt the 'practice road drill' simulation would lead to a checklist haven for those teachers who see the exercise as one of learning to 'look right, then left, etc'. But how could I, in the lesson I actually conducted, know *precisely* either what I intended the children to learn or, after the event, what they did learn? All I can know is that 'a door may have been opened' to an understanding of what failing to keep the Road Safety Code *amounts to*. In talking to the children afterwards, observing their pictures or written accounts, hearing what they tell their parents, or noting their change in attitude towards Road Safety, one might glean what has been understood. But such an emerging picture needs time. Something during the drama, immediately after it, the next day, the next week, or the next term may show itself; or what has been learnt may not be revealed at all. In some cases nothing may have worked for a particular child.

Nevertheless, one persists in trying at least to identify the 'door'. In working with a group of lower adolescents on the topic of cancer I chose the theme of two kinds of 'caring': the professional caring of doctors and nurses and the kind of caring expressed by the family when someone suffers from cancer. I chose this angle as a 'learning area'. I could not foresee what each individual in the class would make of my deliberate juxtaposition within the drama sequence of these two kinds of caring – sometimes the participants were 'in role' as medical staff, at other times as parents of a patient – but I believe there is a greater chance of a door being opened and of the class going through when the teacher knows at least which door it is.

In using the term 'learning area', you should be aware of its limitations. Just as someone does not go to the theatre intent to learn something, weighed down by something called a 'learning area', so in the classroom the learning that goes on is indirect. A participant's focus of attention is primarily on creating an art product (through illustrative/performance activity) or creating a fictitious social context (through dramatic playing). Learning occurs at a level of, to use Polanyi's (1958) useful term, 'subsidiary awareness'.

Thus dramatic activity is always, albeit obliquely, related to knowledge. I have already asserted that this is not the explicit knowledge of skills and facts, but that kind of knowledge related to values, principles, implications and responsibility – what skills and facts *amount to*. The distinction is probably easier to grasp if we talk in terms of 'understanding' rather than 'knowledge'. So often the school context can only think of knowledge in terms of propositional knowledge: a verbal statement about a fact. For instance most six-year olds '*know*' that careless attention to the Road Safety Code can lead to an accident, but this is not to *understand* it. The understanding can only come from direct experience, or from the mediated experience of an art form, one medium being drama.

One problem for the teacher, as you will see in Chapter 7, is that this kind of learning is as intangible as it is significant and, as I have intimated above (p. 115), can take some considerable time to reveal itself. Another problem is what such learning should be called. 'Conceptual' seems to be the most appropriate, but this is often associated with a purely intellectual process. However, I cannot think of anything better, so 'conceptual' will have to do, provided we acknowledge that feelings are engaged in the development of concepts.

Mental skills

Accompanying conceptual learning are a number of mental skills that drama activity continually draws on. The very act of makebelieve is a mental activity in that:

- it requires an 'as if' frame of mind;
- it requires the motivation and the ability to sustain the 'as if';
- it encourages hypothesis before a fictitious event – 'What would happen *if* . . .?', we ask ourselves;

- it encourages 'reading between the lines' of what is being expressed, particularly as we have seen in 'illustrative' work;
- it encourages the anticipation of consequences;
- it requires both the recognition of the logic controlling a social event and the application of that logic to it;
- it encourages weighing up the pros and cons in decision-making;
- it encourages looking at implications after an event;
- it encourages sifting out the values implicit within an action;
- it encourages honest reflection on an event, the careful selection of what should be recorded and *how*, using forms as varied as recalling 'feelings' to categorising 'findings';
- above all it develops the capacity for 'standing outside oneself', seeing one's actions, thoughts and experiences as 'objects' to be reflected upon.

The Russian psychologist, Luria (1959), wrote of two sisters he observed in their play, selecting to play 'at being twins'. It is often assumed that *absorption* is a key feature of dramatic activity but, in fact, *detachment* is of equal importance. This is what Dorothy Heathcote refers to as 'decentring'. It is a double featured process:

- detaching oneself from the content in order to examine it and learn from it;
- detaching oneself from the *theatre form* in order to examine *how* something was achieved.

These are equally important processes in the promotion of learning. Now I shall look at other aims, distinguishable from but not independent of content/form.

Personal growth

For many teachers in the 1950s and 1960s in England, Personal Development was seen as having priority over all other aims. In a sense, of course, education must finally be concerned with development of the person. That being so, we are all advocates of personal development. But, obviously, the pioneers of Personal Development as a philosophy for Drama Education intended a special usage of the term. Their emphasis was on self-expression, personal identity, self-esteem, sensitivity, the 'uniqueness of the individual', and on the maturing process. Such a philosophy was part of the progressive movement in Education but, like all forms of emphasis, it can only be fully understood in terms of what it was countering. In Drama Education,

English pioneers, such as Peter Slade (1954) and Brian Way (1967), were putting forward alternative views of the child, of Education and of drama. This was in reaction to the rigid perception of the child as an empty vessel, education as rote learning and drama as stage performance. Again, like all forms of emphasis, while in the early days there has to be an overstatement of the case in order to attract attention, subsequently such an emphasis outlives its usefulness as its message becomes absorbed by the general educational movement.

It is the *emphasis* that becomes anachronistic, not the truth it promotes. A new emphasis does not necessarily deny the value of its predecessor. Such is the case here. It is clear from the earlier diagram (p. 110) that I am posing *Content/form* as superseding the other three categories, each of which has, at one time or another, claimed prior attention over the others. But that is not to disregard the important role that Personal Growth, Social Development, and Theatre Knowledge, Techniques and Crafts play in Drama Education. Promoters of Personal Development as a philosophy were concerned to identify the affective dimension in the learning process. I hope that the Road Safety lesson (p. 112), for example, demonstrates how the content/form objective is achieved through a feeling/thinking dramatic process. It is the affective component that puts the participant in touch with the significance of things.

It may be that, with the current regrettable political interference in Education, we will need to return to re-emphasising Personal Development, especially in relation to such qualities as independence of mind, curiosity, initiative, self-criticism and responsibility. Just this morning on the radio (November 14, 1990) a past Education Minister and headmaster, Sir Rhodes Boyson, and his colleague launched an appeal for raising standards in Education. When his colleague exclaimed, 'We need to teach the three R's', Sir Rhodes Boyson added, 'Of course, Education is about more than the three R's . . .'. I gave three cheers and anticipated that he was perhaps going to talk about values, developing the whole person, etc., but he continued, 'Education is also vocational and technical.'!

Generally speaking, Personal Development and its associated skills of expression related to language and movement can be seen as an ongoing aim, whatever the more explicit content/form aim may be. In this sense one is *always* promoting self-esteem, creating opportunities for experimentation in expression, putting participants in touch with their feelings, etc. These might be called 'soft' objectives, as opposed to the 'hard' objectives of content/form in relation to a *specific* piece of work. Nevertheless, there are times when Personal Development, especially in responding to evident special needs of an individual, is uppermost in the teacher's mind and takes priority over content/form objectives, for instance: making sure the shy child has the chance to articulate his/her ideas; throwing out a challenge to the glib child; building the stature of the ignored child; drawing in the sceptical child; providing an opening for the unsure child to take the initiative. At such times, of course, T in R is indispensible, for this kind of delicate handling can usually only be managed from *'inside'* the creative process. It is not something that the teacher can attend to with any degree of subtlety from the 'touch-line'. On such occasions, and they are fairly common, content/form objectives may be held in abeyance. It does not matter a bit whether or not the child has a grasp on the central concept; that the drama has created an opportunity for self-advancement is all that is important.

There is a sense in which all conceptual knowledge is bound up with *self*. Whereas pioneers such as Brian Way (1967) saw Drama Education as directly developing self-awareness, my preference is to see such growth in terms of the 'self' being affected reflexively by the content/form, that is in the process of engaging formally with a theme one is brought face-to-face with oneself. It is as if the content/form provides the mirror in which we see ourselves. This is brought home no more forcibly than when watching a comedy in the theatre: the audience's laughter is that of *recognition*.

There is another sense in which 'self' plays a major part in what is being created. I am referring to *self-commitment*. I sometimes say to my classes, 'You cannot do drama unless you "give a little bit of yourself" to it.'. To emphasise this with young adults I will sometimes start a workshop that gives them the chance to share something personal about themselves with the rest of us, and to present the information dramatically. This approach invites them to take a personal risk right at the beginning of the work. I am not recommending to the reader that s/he should rush to his/her classes with this kind of activity in mind – its suitability needs to be carefully judged.

Therapy

Drama Therapy is outside the province of this book, as it is not to be expected that teachers, unqualified in therapy, will be using therapeutic methods. It should be noted, however, that therapy has strong links with-classroom drama practice. Obviously, in terms of *aims*, the focus of therapy is on the individual person, but it is interesting to observe how many of the therapeutic methods also use theatre form. I am thinking particularly of psychodrama and sociodrama, which put the 'protagonist' in a theatrical context using devices such as 'role reversal' and 'alter ego', as one might apply to creating a fictitious context. Of course, the 'content' is not some aspect of the world outside oneself but, rather, the content *is* oneself. The therapy operates with two kinds of intentions: one is to do with gaining insight into oneself, the other provides a 'safe', cathartic context in which one might release the 'pain' that has been buried for some time. The lack of the normal protective 'distancing' guaranteed by the employment of fictitious characterisation, fictitious social context or fictitious event disqualifies this kind of therapy as dramatic art.

Social development

It is not surprising that disciples of the humanist movement in the 1960s and 1970s saw drama as a key strategy for social development. The popularity of 'encounter groups', 'T groups', 'Gestalt group-therapy', etc., stemming from the theoretical work and practice of Rogers (1961), Perls (1969) and Maslow (1954), focused attention on group interaction as a key factor in the maturing process. Drama, essentially an ensemble process, was ripe for plucking. Many teachers, influenced by this movement, started to view drama work solely in terms of *group* behaviour, with special emphasis on group *autonomy*.

I can recall many years ago hearing from a frustrated participant who had attended a weekend Drama course for teachers. The course was conducted by a friend of mine who, believing absolutely in the value of group autonomy, had left the group for the whole weekend to decide 'what they wanted to do'. They never found out! In my earliest days of using the device of 'What do you want to make a play about?', I think I deceived myself into thinking I was following the 'new' humanist philosophy. My *real* reason was that it is very difficult to impose content/form on a group you have never met before. As I was, due to the nature of my job, continually meeting fresh groups, I allowed confusion to grow in the minds of teachers, giving them the impression that 'What do you want to make a play about?' was a necessary part of the method. As a result I often came across a teacher, with a class with which s/he was very familiar, opening up the Drama lesson with this same question. The result was often chaos because the poor teacher had to work entirely spontaneously. The situation was exacerbated because this group-autonomy trend coincided with the assumption that all drama had to 'hit them in the guts'! All of this meant that, except with the most distinguished teachers, the work was doomed to failure. Today when I teach in schools I still occasionally begin in this open-ended way. That is because it suits *me*; it should not be seen as part of some approved methodology.

Again an overemphasis on group dynamics distorted what is nevertheless an important characteristic. Not only does drama rely on group interaction in terms of its product, but part of its uniqueness as a learning context stems from the group processes which assist that learning: it provides a unique opportunity for learning from each other.

Successful drama is dependent on positive interaction between group members. Very often a concensus is needed to move the work on, frequently a group can stimulate or dampen the input of an individual, but above all members of the group have to learn to trust each other, *and* they as a group have to learn to trust *drama*. Adolescents who are at a period in their lives when they avoid self-exposure are, not surprisingly, suspicious of an art form that threatens to do just that. Finally, of course, they have to learn to trust the leader of the drama, the teacher. When any one (or more) of these trusts is absent, then *Social Development* becomes a priority (temporarily a 'hard' objective) and once more overrides any aims to do with content/form.

It is in my experience that the social health of a class can be so negative that Social Development can remain a priority for some considerable time. Obviously one tries to choose both content and form that will enhance that development, but often considerable patience is needed. Because much of the teaching I do is with classes I don't know and/or classes that do not normally do any drama, or who are initially suspicious of my particular approach to drama, I have to content myself with getting the class to trust the novel situation. Sometimes, at the end of one or two lessons, I am not at all sure what they might have learnt in terms of content, but I leave with that positive feeling that comes from recognising that, if we re-meet to work on another project, the necessary degree of trust has now accrued. I have noticed that a recent theoretical writer has little tolerance for this kind of uncertainty from a teacher, in respect of what the class might have actually learnt. I think those of us who are arrogant enough to write books must also have some humility, and appreciate that it is not easy to work in this art form, *as an artist* that is. (To work as an *instructor*, of course, is a very different matter.) Let us never forget that some teachers work under very difficult circumstances, circumstances which may be suffering from destructive group-interaction.

When I teach I am very conscious of the *mood* of a group. Indeed, I find myself responding to the class *as* a group, rather than as a lot of individuals, for the natural dynamics of a group have considerable influence on the group's members: they are often controlled by it. I try to pick up the quality of the 'energy' in a room; I *hear* it rather than see it. (We may differ in this respect: some teachers' perception tends to be visual.) The atmosphere will often guide me in the selection of a focus, and in knowing how to start the lesson sequence. One way in which I differ from many teachers is that, if I am faced with a tricky situation, I assume that I have a better chance to resolve it by getting down to some *drama*, rather than by turning to the ever-popular games or sensitivity exercises. I believe that, by *avoiding* drama, the problem may become exacerbated in the long run, but this is a matter of teacher-style and I have no wish to 'preach' to anyone who has a difficult class.

What I *do* object to is the constant use of games and exercises even when the class is not a problem. Some teachers, especially in North America, seem to bind their students into a routine of preliminary 'warm-up' activities that often turn out to be not so much the hors d'oevre, but the whole meal! These exercises are carried out in the name of group behaviour, but I suspect they are there because both teacher and students find them undemanding, and because those teachers would be hard put to know what to do if they couldn't fill up the time with such activities. I wish 'Theatre Games' had never been invented, and as for 'Theatre Sports' . . .! Neither of these false trails are likely to give a grounding in good Theatre or good classroom practice. That is not to say I would *never* use them. For example if I felt my class had been working so hard recently that they needed a break, I might turn to either of these for light relief.

The choice of content is greatly affected by the group as a whole, and the extent to which the *group* is interested in a theme. What you finish up with is often what the more outspoken *leaders* are interested in, until you know your class well, that is, for then you may be able to do something about the problem. One is often dependent on the energy of those same leaders for getting creativity going. Rare are the times when everyone in a group is equally interested in the same theme and equally prepared to bring the same degree of energy to bear on it. Hopefully, as the drama proceeds, there is a chance that the students will all be 'caught' up in it. Just as often, however, the drama proceeds with some of the class as 'passengers' throughout. Again, because we work in an art form, we cannot expect all our students to 'switch on' just because the timetable says they should!

It is not surprising that I have moved into discussing some of the practical problems stemming from group behaviours. As an art, drama depends upon group interaction between actors, and a group statement by actors. I have made the point before that the approach I recommend for classroom drama requires a *collective* starting point. There is a deliberate avoidance, at first, of individual characterisation, but there is often a very firmly implied or stated 'collective characterisation': 'We are all farmers', or 'architects', or 'cavemen'. Always implicit in this is a sense of *collective responsibility borne by the characters*, which goes beyond the individual responsibility felt by the *participants*. This feature of collective characterisation is particularly marked in respect of the M of E approach. Although to the participants the task set (say designing a museum display related to the Bronze Age) appears to be the focus of attention, the teacher uses the task to build up a collective identity of themselves as a firm or agency of designers. It is as if reflected back from the task are implications to do with the agency's past history, reputation, expertise and responsibility. As the group moves to a second and third task, they experience more and more a sense of who they are and what their responsibility is. But more than that, the teacher tries to open up the designers' way of seeing the world: what your eyes tend to pick out if you are a designer; what your priorities tend to be; what you keep and what you discard; what your job *means*. In other words the teacher, in using the M of E approach, attempts to open up for the pupils a whole value system governing expertise.

Theatre knowledge, techniques and crafts

Even as I begin this category, I wonder whether it will be too readily seen as something separate from *Content/form*. Recent theorists and official 'working parties' seem to want to make theatre knowledge and techniques the basis of classroom drama. However, I am cheered by Andy Kempe's *The GCSE Drama Coursebook* (1990). The intention behind this text for older adolescents is clearly to sustain the content/form concept in the minds of the young people as they work. Each page is rich in material, issues and themes to be transformed into drama. Text work and non-text work are interdependent, and the three main strands *running parallel* to each other – 'making plays', 'putting on plays' and 'understanding plays' – give further coherence to the notion that substance and form are interrelated. The skills and knowledge about theatre involved are to be acquired *in context*. Each section requires the students to respond to a piece of text and to create work of their own related to a similar theme (not necessarily in that order). This is how the author describes content/form to GCSE students:

> People often describe things as being dramatic. 'All the world's a stage' they say, as if all the things that happen in it are deliberately planned, as they are in a stage play. But there is a difference between the 'dramas' that happen in the everyday world and drama which is deliberately created to understand and reflect that world. The type of drama you are studying starts with an idea or feeling. It then has to be shaped and moulded into something that others will understand.
>
> Think of a cake. You will already have a clear idea of what cakes are all about, so if you were to ask to go away and make one you'd know that you would need a number of ingredients and a recipe. Just

> having the ingredients on their own won't do. If you mix them together in the wrong order or wrong proportions, what you'll end up with won't be very cakey. . . .
>
> . . . Like a cake, drama is a blend of **content** and **form**. The **content** of a drama is what is in it, what it's all about – its ingredients. The **form** is what makes it drama as opposed to anything else – its recipe.

This is a fine way of making it quite clear to young people that learning about drama is not a matter of concentrating on skills. The relationship of content to form is laid out clearly in the book's introduction, there are constant reminders of content/form throughout the text, and the way the chapters are organised focuses attention on *skills to be learnt within the content/form context.*

For instance Project 2 in Chapter 2 is called 'Relationships and conflict'. Here the students are required to look at the skills related to building a character. After some useful exercises that draw attention to *relationships* between characters, the work moves quickly into the close examination of part of the Athol Fugard text, *Master Harold . . . and the Boys*. This is followed by trying out contrasting ways of performing this small excerpt and looking more closely at the issue embedded in the text. Then, having charted their ideas, the students are invited to create, through improvisation or writing, a scene of their own which would further illuminate how society can put pressure on a minority. Further reflection takes them into considering other plays, Films, or TV dramas that seem to deal with this same theme. They are asked, particularly, to consider such examples in terms of the victimised character.

This seems to me to be an ideal way of working in content/form/technique/theatre knowledge, with pupils taking an examination in Drama. That it is a *course*book naturally has its limitations: there is no teacher available to change the sequence or content to suit the needs of the class and there is no chance for the teacher to take on the occasional role in order to enhance the pupils' work. The wise teacher, of course, will overcome this apparent deficiency and use the material of the book in a way that *serves* rather than *binds* the class.

Many of the skills and much of the knowledge identified in Kempe's book (1990) are those related to what I have called 'theatre elements'. These were discussed on p. 114. But, as one would expect for an examination class, many of the theatre crafts are also included: lighting, design, mask-making, etc. Each of these is to be practised 'in context' as part of content and form, with opportunities for individual students to follow further specialist paths as part of their project work. I would suggest such specialisms could be extended to include *Commedia dell'arte* type of comedy, the mask-making and clowning improvisational experimentation of Keith Johnstone (1981), and Theatre-in-Education programmes. In connection with the latter, I recently had the opportunity to see a programme on Child Sexual Abuse, devised and performed by fifteen/sixteen-year old Drama students under the guidance of their Drama teacher and the School Health Counselling Service for an audience of nine-year olds. The performers toured several British Columbian Elementary Schools in Victoria. The effectiveness of this programme was measured by the number of children in very real need who immediately took advantage of the personal counselling offered after each performance. It seems to me that this kind of programme is an ideal way of giving older adolescents an experience of 'purposeful theatre'.

Kempe's book is directed at sixteen-year olds, examination classes in particular. It is my purpose in this book to try to ensure that all pupils are given a basic grounding throughout their school life in the art form of theatre. One outcome, but not the most important, will be that sixteen-year olds will take sophisticated text-work and performance in their stride. In addition to the theatre elements already discussed, a number of techniques will be exercised continually from an early age. These may include use of voice, use of movement, techniques related to 'illustrating', directing, making a coherent social context, 'reading' a depiction, reading a text for 'subtext', responding spontaneously to each other, responding to T in R, etc. Unfortunately there are those who, guided by some recent theorists in the field, will automatically seize such a list and start teaching 'to' it. Such techniques should be *embedded* in content/form (they are all there in my sample sequences of lessons in Chapter 5). However, some teachers will find a way of extracting them from any context and will see them as the equivalent of five-finger exercises, matters for instruction and drill. There will be no one around to tell them what harm they are doing, for even officially appointed 'working party' committees seem to be allowing themselves to be led by the nose in this respect, at least if recent 'working papers' and other official documents are anything to go by. Further, because many of these techniques are related to the performance mode, these same teachers are likely to drop any truly existential experiencing. Again, this is given tacit support by the DES (1989) whose writing gains in confidence when it speaks of dressing-up clothes, electric torches and percussion instruments, as well as '... stage sets, properties, costumes, make-up, stage lighting ...' (*Drama from 5 to 16*, p. 11) as giving support to techniques of public performance. There is no guidance here as to the maturity of the pupils, just an indiscriminate recommendation to teachers teaching all ages.

However, whereas in *Drama from 5 to 16* the DES (1989) appeared to welcome formal and informal performances by children, their more recent document (1990) does concede that all may not be well:

> In most schools greater emphasis was given to drama at certain times of the year. Christmas, and to a lesser extent Easter, and the festivals and events of faiths other than Christianity were often celebrated in ways which gave a boost to drama. In some schools this was not always a good thing either for drama or for the understanding and enjoyment of the events themselves. This was mainly because they were over-rehearsed, resulting in a stilted, tightly prescribed production.
>
> Similarly, where classes took turns to conduct assemblies which often incorporated a dramatic presentation, the work was sometimes viewed by the class teacher as an onerous chore requiring much rehearsal and time-consuming effort for little return. In these circumstances the participation rate for many of the children was low, so that too few members of the class really became involved to a serious extent in the performance; the others sat for long periods waiting to take part or simply watched the others rehearse. (Paragraphs 9 & 10)

I have my doubts whether this recent qualification will have much influence on current Arts in schools or Arts Council thinking, for people read what they *want* to read and there is at the moment a vested interest in child performance. This has something to do with the fact that most advisers on official committees are not practising teachers. Perhaps more relevant is the present political climate (I am not talking here of *Party* politics). We are living in a time when the establishment is desperate to go back to 'Education as instruction'. The result is that educational writers in all fields, including drama, are hedging their bets by describing classroom activities in terms that could conceivably be seen as 'instructing in techniques', should that become the new fashion! It is a pity that new faces on the drama scene have not the courage of Peter Slade, Brian Way or Dorothy Heathcote, who were prepared to stand *against* current trends.

It is my belief that development in the basic theatre elements, as described on p. 114, will ensure that our pupils will be able to approach any aspect of Theatre intelligently and perceptively, not least in respect of responding to the work of dramatists. Unfortunately, the limitations of our culture and educational system often reduce this experience to play-texts rather than to play performances. Rare are the oportunities for our pupils to visit the theatre. Many never see any professional theatre. At least television can sometimes supply good examples of play performance, but under the present economic and Philistine regime, even this possibility is continually being threatened. A serious extension of this exists in the lack of opportunity for *teachers* to see much live theatre. This must inevitably lead to Drama teaching that fails to be sustained by the very source that should be its inspiration.

7 Assessment

I have been among those who have eschewed writing about methods of assessment in drama; anyone having the stamina to comb through my previous books or articles would search in vain for the subject to be given any more than a passing reference. Such neglect does not mean that I have no ideas on the subject. Indeed, that could not be possible, since in my classroom practice I (like every other teacher) apply criteria for assessment continually as a necessary part of the work. I simply haven't felt that I have anything to add to common practice among Drama teachers, just as I haven't felt inclined to give advice to Drama specialists about putting on a school play, important as that is. Likewise I have avoided sounding knowledgeable about 'play corners' in early schooling (I understand a great deal *less* than most reception teachers about this activity). The study of dramatic texts for examination purposes, and even puppetry, might also be added to a quite lengthy list of important classroom activities linked with drama that I have failed to discuss. I make no apologies for this neglect; most writing on education is skewed in the direction of whatever seems in need of elaboration at any one time. However, I have discovered that this 'sin of omission' sometimes seems to give people the impression that neglected aspects are not worthy of attention. In striving to develop an understanding of dramatic playing activity as a structured experience, I have been reacting against two philosophical extremes: the old view that child drama was a matter of 'free' play and the still common assumption that drama activity is to do either with the analysis of texts or with training children as performers ready for the school play.

Some braver souls have already published work on assessment (using the term broadly to include evaluation and attainment targets), but generally speaking their writings suffer from one or more of four critical weaknesses:

1 As I read their advice I cannot 'see' children. That is they are not drawing on classroom practice as they write, but rather on some philosophical or aesthetic theories to do with making judgements *about* classroom practice.

2 They are too keen (often for political reasons) to find theories that embrace *all* the Arts, verbal and non-verbal. They are like a family of farmers desperately trying to cover a haystack with a tarpaulin that is not quite big enough, so that as they pull it in one direction another part of the stack becomes exposed. But as long as they just look at the covered area in front of them, they feel confident that the stack is waterproofed.

3 Even those few writers who choose to confine their attention to *drama* only are often writing from a narrow frame of reference. They turn out to be from a College of Higher Education, from the professional theatre or from the Drama department of a Comprehensive School. Instead of discussing the assessment of drama with reference to what they know most about, their own practice, they purport to speak for a wide range of educational experience in drama. Without turning a hair, an ex-College of Higher Education practitioner will often advise on Primary School practice and its assessment. What is offered, of course, is a distorted perspective on what should be done with younger children. Working backwards from their knowledge of Secondary or Higher Education practice, they assume that younger children should be involved in a watered-down version of the same, that young children are 'little adolescents' and that their drama experience should amount to a preparation for performance theatre. Working parties and appointed committees trying to offer the public an 'official line' on drama should be wary of their members, whose background may be very limited and yet whose current standing may be influential.

4 Some Drama specialists writing about assessment still see drama practice almost entirely in terms of *acting skills*, and believe that, ultimately, 'success' is about playing 'big parts' in school productions. Too readily young adolescents are taught quick acting tricks and superficial techniques that, if they do pursue an acting career, have to be *unlearned* when they get to Theatre School. Yet their assessment record may show high grades, given for the veneer of ability the students have acquired. I was talking recently to a Head of Drama in a Senior High School in Vancouver, British Columbia. She had in one of her Drama classes a student who was picked for a leading role in a film. At fifteen years of

age he now felt he had passed the supreme test of ability in drama and did not do any more work on the course. His conception of the course was that it was about being a performer and that he had already reached that particular attainment target!

Some of the principal issues

I shall attempt, towards the end of this chapter, to offer a framework for assessment, but first it is necessary to look in detail at some of the issues. There is one I have continually raised, that of 'learning through drama', but there are others. For instance how does one assess dramatic playing behaviour? Most discussion of assessment seems to assume illustrative/performance behaviour. Even more of a tease is the problem presented to an assessor when the teacher is 'in role'! And what about 'theatre elements' in the dramatic playing work of young children – what is one looking for in terms of assessment? I shall take each of these thorny issues in turn.

Assessment of dramatic playing behaviour

I argued in Chapter 2 that the dramatic playing activity is initially about creating a social context, just as in any 'life' situation. Following an ethnomethodological perspective, I suggested that in everyday social situations we 'work at' (often unconsciously) making the context we want, so that we can give the social event a suitable label, such as 'a meeting', 'a chat about old times', 'an interview with the boss', etc. Then we often *evaluate* such an event: we speak of a 'good' meeting, a 'successful' interview or a 'pleasurable' chat. This is done on the assumption that the event actually existed and that we have a set of criteria by which we can make judgements objectively.

Although it is recognised that the participants have to *work* to create a social event, it does not follow that it exists only in their minds. There is, in fact, a 'product': a meeting, a chat or an interview. An outside observer could reasonably identify the product according to the actions of the participants. The reason for this is that the only means the participants have of making anything is through the public media of action and language. The *meaning* of what is going on lies in the created product.

This 'making a social context' provides the basis for dramatic playing, and therefore for initial assessment. The product is dependent on the participants' having the appropriate resources. These resources are the public media of expression – the actions and language that logically belong to the implicit rules of whatever social event is being created. For example doing drama about 'hospitals' requires the participants to engage in appropriate 'hospital' actions and language. As discussed in Chapter 2, this first step in makebelieve appears to rely on a degree of imitation of the world, especially in its initial stages. One might therefore expect assessment to be straightforward: 'Do they or do they not achieve some resemblance to "hospital behaviour"?'. Any answer to this question might need to be quite strongly qualified, for a number of reasons:

1 The students' knowledge of hospitals may be inadequate by any reasonable adult standard.
2 Their commitment to this particular drama may be low.
3 An individual in the group may be undermining the work.
4 Although the context is labelled 'hospital', this is but a springboard for another theme, 'hospital' seeming not to be integral to the work.

Either singly or in combination, these kinds of factors raise many questions relating to assessment. I shall discuss each of these points below:

1 If we felt there was an external standard by which we could measure the acceptable degree of resemblance to the 'real' world of hospitals, then anything less would be judged as below that standard. This would be absurd, for knowledge of this kind is relative. Even a 'reasonable adult standard' falls short of a nurse's or consultant's conception of hospital. Likewise a young child's knowledge is likely to be very limited (although I did once in the middle of doing drama on this particular topic discover that we had a son of a surgeon in the class – he took over!). It seems then that, in making a judgement about the success with which a group is 'making' a fictitious social context, we have to conjecture what that group might be expected to know. If, for instance, they were five-years olds we might make a generous allowance. On the other hand, if they were a GCSE examination group involved in creating theatre about hospitals as an examination project, which included performing an excerpt from Peter Nicholls' *National Health* and creating their own 'hospital' drama, then one would expect them to have done adequate research into the subject. Indeed, evidence of their research could be included in their examination folder.

2 We can see that, whereas in respect of point 1 the age level of the class is likely to affect the final assessment, lack of commitment to either

drama itself or to the particular subject matter may be a characteristic of any age group. Indeed, I have found school headteachers or principals (or any group where people are anxious to preserve their image) among the most uncommitted groups I have worked with! In practice a distinction has to be drawn between a group that is generally uncommitted, in which case their work will be considered below target, and a group which has lost its commitment to the particular work in hand (perhaps the students have tired of it, failed to become inspired by it, taken on more than they bargained for or, as I shall discuss later, the teacher has structured the work inadequately), in which case, this attitude being untypical of the group, assessment might be waived for that piece of work.

3 It will be noticed that, in talking about assessment in Drama, I am making two assumptions: that achievement in terms of content/form is an immediate issue, and that there is an ensemble responsibility. If we agree that there is a product to be assessed, then we must also agree that it is a collective enterprise. But just as in the 'life' situation a 'meeting' or a 'party' may not be successful because of the detracting behaviour of a minority or individual, so in drama-making one or two can let down the group, either because of recalcitrant behaviour or because of inadequate resources. We all know what it is like to have a young child, in the middle of a drama about Stone Age people, make a reference to watching the television. At such times the teacher makes a swift diagnosis of the cause: Is it that the child really doesn't know, or is s/he enjoying upsetting the fiction? S/he also calculates the extent to which the rest of the class is going to be 'thrown' by the inappropriate remark. Indeed, the way the class recovers from the hiatus will be part of the teacher's ultimate assessment of the work. Whether it does or not will often depend on the status of the defaulting member within the natural social hierarchy of the class. If s/he is a natural leader, recovery is less likely. And, of course, any final assessment might well discriminate against that particular child, just as the discrimination will be in favour of the child who helps the rest of the class to a quick recovery. Again, just as in the 'life' situation, one is grateful to the individual who 'saves' the meeting or the party. However, one has to be wary – such situations are rarely black and white. The 'destructive' child in question may be justified in upsetting the fiction, and the teacher may be too blinkered to recognise that it is that particular child's way of protesting, say, that the work lacks integrity. I shall return to the question of assessment of collaborative work at the end of this chapter (p. 143).

4 The meaning of any social event operates at many different levels. A wedding, for example, will be about many different things according to one's perspective. For the bride and groom, that it is a wedding is central to the experience. This may not be the case for the 'revellers' towards the end of the wedding party. For some people a wedding may be about new friendships struck or enmity reconfirmed. I recently watched a wedding party outside a church in Padua, Italy, where the two sides engaged in a fight that had to be controlled by the police! When young people create a *drama* about a wedding, it sometimes happens that it slides into being about something else, the 'wedding' simply lapsing in importance. This raises questions about the validity of what they are creating, for the art form of drama is dependent on its themes being bound up with the particularity of the context. The theme may centre on revels, new friendships or a fight, but the 'wedding' must somehow remain integral to those themes for it to have dramatic value. In the exploratory approach of dramatic playing it often happens that the drama imperceptibly moves away from its original starting point. When this happens the participants need to have their attention drawn to what is happening, if they do not already realise it. Then they must make a choice between re-establishing the original context or theme and treating the new context as a new beginning. If they begin to stray a second time, this could be considered to be an indiscipline within the group, and the students would be assessed accordingly.

So far I have implied that making a social event in drama is a matter of sending the 'right' signals to each other, for example in the hospital context, doing and saying 'hospital' by: miming appropriate actions; speaking appropriate technical dialogue; demonstrating a respect for hospital hierarchy; creating a mood of dealing with life-and-death matters, etc. Some or all of these may be necessary for the participants to make the context believable to themselves. These are the necessary *descriptive* activities characteristic of the early stages of most social events. The teacher making an assessment does so by bearing in mind the four qualifications listed on p. 131.

There is a *second* phase to the dramatic playing mode, a kind of 'gear changing' when the participants move from the 'descriptive' to the 'existential'. When this happens the pupils no longer feel they have to work at making the context believable and real: it *feels* real and *they can submit themselves to it*; they *trust* it; they are free to enjoy its riches; they may find that they draw on resources and talents they did not know they had, and have new insights into what the drama is about. This is the power of the existential moment: it is alive, fluid, open to spontaneous invention and charged with energy. When it is over, however brief it has been, you will have a feeling that you were the author of something real, something authentic, and you will learn by reflecting on it.

Regretfully, as I said in Chapter 2 (p. 12), many pupils go through their whole schooling without ever having this experience. Many *teachers* who teach Drama have never had a true 'dramatic playing' experience, so do not know what to look for. Many theorists will glibly admit some value to what they often choose to call 'improvisation', without realising that this can be *either* descriptive or existential. Indeed, in North American schools where 'Theatre Sports' have caught on, 'improvisation' in *some* courses has become reduced to 'How slickly entertaining can you be with a mere half minute's preparation time?'. The DES (1990) draws a distinction between 'play', 'role-play' and 'performance'. The difference seems to be one of degrees of formality. There is no acknowledgement of any qualitative differences in acting behaviours. Perhaps it is because they never have the chance to *see* the 'change of gear' I am talking about although, in reading their interesting samples of lessons, one can only assume that part of the success of these exercises lay in the fact that the pupils were, for some of the time at least, operating existentially. I concede, of course, that the two modes can become merged in a way that sometimes leads to inappropriate criteria being applied, as in the example from the work on Pinter's *The Room*, described at the end of Chapter 2 (p. 28).

Of course, dramatic playing like any other dramatic form may be of inferior quality. Much that is done in the name of existential experiencing is unworthy and time-wasting. However, we need to understand where the teacher's responsibility lies in respect of the assessment of both descriptive and existential drama. The insightful teacher must be able to recognise when the class is ready to 'shift gear' from the descriptive to the existential. S/he will need to note the extent to which different members of his/her group are able to 'submit' to the fictitious context once it has been made believable. S/he will then observe how effective they are in respect of:

- inventing within the established logic of the context;
- interacting within the group;
- extending their skills, particularly in relation to language and movement;
- responding to T in R (if it is occurring);
- handling the art form.

The first three of these are obvious areas of assessment; the last two need further explanation.

Assessment when the teacher is 'in role'

Whether or not a child can respond to a teacher's role will depend very much on how well the role is set up. I do not mean, of course, how convincingly a character is portrayed but, rather, how securely the ground is laid for the introduction of such a role, and how clearly the idea illustrated by the role is conveyed, for T in R behaviour is invariably *descriptive*. An inadequate response by the pupils may be the teacher's fault entirely.

I can recall working with a group of examination pupils in a London Comprehensive School who were studying Ibsen's *An Enemy of the People*. The two sessions of drama I was to conduct were to be filmed by the ILEA camera team. I drew up a careful plan, using the metaphor of a psychiatric hospital. Here the central character in Ibsen's play (Dr Stockmann) was to be subjected to a psychiatric investigation, using psychodrama, by the hospital staff. Members of the class played both hospital staff and other characters in Stockmann's personal and professional life. I was in role as the senior consultant. The *idea* was a good one, but I carried it out in terms of my plan instead of in terms of the class. The students did not know the text as well as I had been led to expect; they were scared of the cameras but anxious to do well in front of them; they were perplexed by this new drama teacher and bewildered by his idea of setting up a psychiatric hospital. Instead of adapting the sequence of their experiences, including my use of T in R, to the readiness of the class, and instead of back-tracking when I discovered where they really were in relation to the work, I relentlessly pursued my plan.

Afterwards, I tended to blame the class for not knowing the text, but of course the whole point of the teacher 'in' and 'out of role' is that s/he should adapt the material to suit what is happening. I could easily have set up a series of preliminary experiences that would have allowed the pupils to gain confidence in themselves and in the metaphor, before moving to the major experience within the plan. I failed the class. They still pulled out some good work, but it was not based on an early foundation of trust. So how do we assess our pupils' ability in this kind of circumstance? Do we give the pupils low grades because the teacher set the work up ineptly, or give them high grades because they did well *in spite of* the teacher?!

Having said this, it is still possible to assess a child's general ability in responding to the teacher's contribution. Assuming that what the teacher offers is well-timed, appropriately prepared for and clearly signalled, then differences between the pupils' responses may emerge. The most responsive children in drama will be able to 'read' the teacher's role at a level that goes beyond the 'plot'. Bruner (1971) demonstrated how young children respond to comic strips at differing levels of generality. While some can only respond in terms of 'what happens next', others are able to see social or psychological implications. The same applies to T in R which is open to being 'read' at both a surface level and in response to the true 'centre' of what the teacher is offering. The teacher who 'in role' muses, 'Do we have the right to make judgements about people who are worse off than we are?', isn't simply slowing down the decision-making, but is opening up the possibility of philosophical reflection. The dialogue from teacher to young children, 'Suppose we never return? . . . That's my front door there . . . suppose I never go through it again?', is an attempt to 'deepen' the implications of going on some risky adventure that the class seems to be taking very lightly. Those children who can respond to this new tack introduced by the teacher, and who can further what the teacher has started, are likely to get more out of the drama. It is as though the teacher has moved into a minor key, inviting the pupils to follow. Thus any assessment relates to the child's capacity for seeing the potential, at many different levels, in what the teacher is offering. I call this 'reading', for it has strong links with a child's capacity for reading comic strips, pictures *and* the printed page. Effective T in R raises the standard of what is to be 'read'. As I have already emphasised above, the children's ability is dependent on the effectiveness of their fellow artist, the teacher, whose input has to be well-timed and appropriate. The teacher has to sense the 'right' comment and the 'right' question. Morgan and Saxton in their fascinating book (1991) draw the reader's attention to the importance of selecting just the 'right' kind of question and the 'right' style of delivering it.

This process of raising the standard of what is created by appropriate teacher-input is not, of course, confined to dramatic activity. Recently I was watching my granddaughter, Claire, struggling at the age of five to do 'plucking' exercises on her newly acquired violin. She was managing adequately by carefully counting to find the right rhythm and strike the right strings. But when her father provided an exciting 'backing', the piece was 'lifted' into a musical event, and what had been from Claire mechanically correct, now made musical sense. Her whole body expressed the rhythm and she and her father together created music. Her father was doing the equivalent of T in R by enhancing the musical experience. This is what Vygotski (1978) calls the 'zone of proximal development': the development that occurs when the input by an adult helps the learner to achieve beyond their previous capacity.

There are many aspects of the dramatic playing activity that teacher and pupils together will be concerned to assess from day to day. Language, speech and movement are the means by which ideas and dramatic forms are explored. Economy, authenticity and inventiveness are some of the criteria by which one tests standards in these expressive forms.

Assessment of 'illustrative/performance' behaviour

This is, of course, relatively easier to handle than the dramatic playing mode, as the acting behaviour is entirely descriptive. Again, it centres on a combination of form and content. The question the teacher is continually posing is related to the effectiveness of what is being expressed, both in terms of the clarity of ideas and of their expression through the ensemble presentation. A high standard of effectiveness requires that ideas are *uniquely* expressed, that is that the meaning is embedded in the form.

The repertoire of theatre elements already discussed (p. 114) is just as relevant to the illustrative activity as to dramatic playing. Again, such features as tension and manipulation of space are an *ensemble* responsibility. *Repeatability* is also a characteristic of this 'instant coffee' kind of work. It is not unusual for a teacher or the rest of the class to request, 'Can we see that again?', with a view to re-discussing emerging ideas or re-perceiving subtleties previously missed.

The work is always done for someone else to view. This brings in the responsibility of the *audience* who may act as the 'director' as well as viewers. This introduces what is perhaps a new feature of assessment: it should be assumed that the audience are also working and consequently the way they behave – in offering comments, asking questions, analysing their perceptions, making recommendations, etc. – should be subjected to assessment, whatever the age group concerned. The 'director's eye' and the 'audience member's eye' need to be developed from an early age.

The end-product of illustrative activity is relatively easy to make judgements about, but one wonders to what extent a teacher should take into account the ups and downs of the groups' exploring and rehearsing processes. Sometimes the final piece of work is not what the group is capable of because the participants have submitted to an uncomfortable compromise in the name of concensus. Sometimes the teacher knows that one group is suffering a destructive 'passenger' or an overbearing leader. Alternatively it has been known for a group to have one member whose acting ability is so mesmerising that inadequate work by the others passes unnoticed! These group-dynamic problems are daily teasers for the teacher committed to making honest assessments.

Learning through drama

How do we find out what has been learnt? As I pointed out in Chapter 6 (p. 115), in matters to do with understanding rather than with knowledge of skills or facts we are dependent on subtle clues over a period of time. What the pupils have begun to understand they may be unable to articulate, and yet an important shift in the direction of new understanding may have occurred. One can appreciate why some current theorists and practitioners wish to confine appraisal to acting skills, theatre crafts and textual study – they are so much more easily definable and recognisable. But this is to deny why we are doing drama in the first place. Drama must be about engaging with something that matters, and the degree to which our understanding is extended in the art experience is paramount. As assessors we may be guided by the way the pupils are ready to stand apart from their work and *reflect* on what they are creating, either during the process of making it or after it has been made. The reflection may take the form of talking, writing or visual expression; we may also pick up clues from the way pupils apply their new understanding in a different dramatic or 'life' context. Obviously this applies to many different kinds of drama practice, but I suspect that, because T in R is continually initiating new levels of meaning-making, identification of what the pupils are understanding is particularly hazardous. Sometimes, of course, the teacher can create occasions for reflection *during* the work, breaking off from time to time to test the pupils' grasp on the implications of any 'change of gear'. On the other hand, in the M of E approach there is always evidence of the standard of achievement, for by its very nature this method necessitates *recording* what the participants are doing.

The child's ability to handle the elements of theatre – the child as artist

The significance of the teacher's contribution 'in role' is not, of course, solely a matter of substance: such a contribution should enhance the art of *Theatre*. The teacher may inject elements of Theatre that are absent from the children's own work. Again the question is: 'To what extent can these children 'pick up' and sustain the theatrical element offered through the teacher's role?'.

Important as it is for children to be able to respond to teacher-input, I now turn to a consideration of children's ability to *initiate* dramatic form without the help of the teacher.

About four years ago when my elder granddaughter, Helen, was four-years old, she was scolded by her mother for trying to insist that she ate a Mars bar before her meal. She re-enacted the incident by putting me 'in role' as a 'naughty boy' who must not touch the Mars bar on the shelf behind him. (There was no bar, nor was there a shelf.) As my hand crept in the direction of the supposed shelf, she enjoyed arresting my arm in its progress and delivering a vehement reprimand. After a few times she changed to standing a few metres away and, on each occasion, rushed forward to check her 'naughty boy'. She then discovered (I did not prompt her in any way, I simply, passively, continued the action she wanted me to make) that turning her back on me, pretending to walk away and, finally, appearing to head for the door, all progressively enhanced the excitement of 'catching me in the act'.

This is what I mean by 'understanding' dramatic form. Her's, of course, was not an intellectual understanding; she was probably not conscious of what she was doing, let alone articulate about it. We can only guess at how many similar contexts she would have gone through before she would have stopped 're-inventing the wheel', that is before she could jump straight to the dramatic final step without going through the preliminary exploratory steps. Nevertheless, she demonstrated a knowledge of Theatre shared with dramatists, directors and actors: she selected a clearly defined focus that enabled her to have the experience she wanted; she utilised the difference in status between the two 'characters'; she increased tension by delaying the moment of excitement (arresting my arm); she built tension by manipulating space significantly; and she understood the playwright's art of creating the 'unexpected' by leading my character to be duped by her character's imminent departure – all this in the particularity of the 'forbidden Mars bar/disobedient child context'. The meaning of the experience lies in the content/form combination.

Thus in the pre-school child there is the potential for the very basis of Theatre. The previous anecdote, illustrating as it does the 'existential' mode, demonstrates the manipulation of time and space, the application of constraint, the development of tension, contrast between characters and an element of surprise. I believe most pre-school children have this ability in Theatre. Unfortunately, this natural understanding is often and inevitably allowed to atrophy in the formal school situation. There are a number of reasons for this, listed below:

1 Such activity is left to unstructured play and is not seen by the observing teacher as important.

2 If drama is introduced into the classroom it is often confined to 'illustrative/performance' activity.

3 To expect the child who knows how to harness Theatre in his/her solitary or one-to-one play (as was the case in the anecdote), and to utilise that same knowledge in small or large-group drama, is to expect the impossible. The new dimension of 'groupness' represents a huge factor

> militating against the individual child's natural creativity. This is not a reason for disbanding drama as a large-group activity, but it is a reason for teachers to realise that the children will hold their natural skills in abeyance unless they can be *eased into* the group dramatic process. T in R as a device is almost essential if dramatic playing is to have dramatic form. Once the children realise that this form coincides with the theatre resources they already possess, they will move confidently towards taking the initiative in a large group.

This takes time, however, and groups will vary. Assessment in the Infant School will relate to where the pupils are in this process of re-learning dramatic art form. Sadly, some teachers do harness children's natural understanding of Theatre, but in the wrong direction – they encourage the manipulation of time and space and the creation of tension, etc. as part of the young child's *performance* repertoire. As I have said before (p. 129), some influential Comprehensive and Higher Education teachers believe that training young children to perform in public is what drama should be about (and some infant teachers are ready to listen to them). It is so much easier to get young children to jump through performance hoops (I *know*, because this is how I started to teach Drama!) than to create a rich environment of learning through whole-class dramatic playing. And, let's face it, teacher-education institutions may not be helping them to know how to do this.

Finding a framework for assessment

In this and in previous chapters I have emphasised the value of drama as a medium for conceptual learning. At the same time I drew attention to some limitations of such a notion. It is difficult to tell:

- exactly *what* has been learnt;
- what *duration* of time is involved;
- what *quality* of learning is occurring.

I also pointed out that the participants must not be burdened with the requirement to learn something (p. 116). In other words, although in an educational context a teacher is expected to take full advantage of the learning potential for his/her pupils, the focus for the participants, it appears, is on 'making drama' – creating a product. I have slipped in 'it appears' because the phrase, 'making drama', could be misleading, for it could be construed as offering a way of looking at drama in the classroom as an *alternative* to learning and understanding. There is indeed a danger, in confirming that the participants' goal is 'making drama', that some teachers will interpret this as inviting either free play or theatre skills empty of content.

'Making drama' is just what our pupils *are* doing, but there is also a sense in which drama-making is inescapably linked with learning, understanding and knowledge. We have to find a way of combining the two, a concept that may *imply* an openness to conceptual learning or a change of understanding without that being an explicit *requirement*. It would *also imply* a search for dramatic form. I am suggesting that the phrase 'Drama for meaning-making' might be useful in this context.

Drama for meaning-making

Such a phrase allows the teacher to continue to think in terms of 'What are they learning?'. It steers the participants unequivocally towards content that is important to them, and it also puts *drama* first.

I believe this provides a more secure base-line, for concepts related to 'learning' and 'change of understanding' can now remain as possible sub-categories of 'meaning-making'. While the assessor may or may not have assessable evidence of 'change of understanding' in some of the participants (it will be taken into account if such evidence is there), s/he must *expect* evidence of attention given by the participants to *the making of meaning*, for meaning-making is what all dramatic activity is about.

We readily make assumptions about 'meaning making' when we read, watch or give a critique of a play. We may explicitly or implicitly ask the question, 'What is the meaning here in this art product?'. Of course, to the question put in this way the answer is always the same: 'The meaning *is* the art product.'. So, in order to reflect as we read, watch or criticise, we shift the order of the question to something like, 'What *kind* of meanings do we have here in this art product?', or 'Is there a coherent whole?', or 'Does the product make me think?'. These are some of the legitimate questions any theatre-goer or professional critic may ask. They are also legitimate questions in respect of the dramatic 'meaning-making' in the classroom. Thus in classroom assessment you might ask:

- What kind of meanings are there here?
- Is the context created credible to the participants (and to an audience where there is one)?
- Are these kinds of meaning sufficiently significant to the participants?
- Is there evidence of intellectual effort?
- Does what has been created have coherence for the participants (and for an audience where there is one)?
- Does the drama make *me* think?

There is a second type of question the theatre critic poses, related to *theatrical form* – the *how* of the meaning-making:

- What aesthetic forms, metaphor, conventions, styles, genres, characters, focus, context and setting does the playwright employ as vehicles for meaning-making?

These too are legitimate questions to be asked of work in the classroom:

- *How* do these pupils set about making meaning?
- *How* do they negotiate meanings?
- *How* do they sustain and refine them?

In classroom assessment there are two sources of evidence to be taken into account: the 'product' – the drama created – and the 'process' – the experience of the group in achieving the product. Of the 'process' one might ask, for example, 'Did they try out alternative stage-positions for their 'narrator'?' (theatre form) or, 'Did they do any reading round the subject or bring in source material?' (content). Thus the 'what' and the 'how' of meaning-making can be related to both form and content. But, of course, there is a further division to be taken into account: 'Drama for meaning-making' can relate just as much to dramatic playing behaviour as to illustrative/performance behaviour. It is also possible to see dramatic playing both as process and product. Typical 'how' questions for dramatic playing might be: 'Did they take into account ideas offered tentatively, or were they just influenced by the most forceful members of the group?' (process), and 'How did they manage to disguise their suspicions of the disloyal family?' (product). Notice that 'process' questions tend to relate to the participants' experience, whereas 'product' questions relate to the fiction.

I am suggesting that *Drama for meaning-making* can provide us with a coherent framework from which to operate assessment. In the *broadest terms* the following questions would be posed:

Questions related to content:

- What kinds of meanings are here?
- Is there evidence of conceptual learning?

Questions related to form:

- *How* have these kinds of meaning been achieved?
- Is there evidence of cognitive and social skills (thinking, questioning, listening to each other, etc.) being acquired?

In each case these questions should be applied to:

- process and product;
- dramatic playing and illustrating/performing.

The process of assessment is hugely complex. I hope that the above suggested framework will provide a base-line that will cater for a wide range of dramatic activities. Many of the issues discussed earlier in this chapter should now fall into place within this frame.

'Grading' a group

I tend to follow a particular procedure for grading group work which the reader may be interested in. I am sure other teachers have methods that are just as useful, but I thought there was no harm in sharing what I do.

There are many times when, as the examiner or as the teacher, I am presented with the end-product of a group's work, work which has perhaps taken several weeks to prepare. As examiner, of course, it is probable that I do not know the participants. I begin by making a private categorisation of the *product*. I assess what I see of the outcome by giving the work, say, a C if that is assumed by the institution to be average, an A if I thought it was distinguished, and a D if I thought it was less than satisfactory, etc.

I invite the students (before they see my grades) to grade each other, using the criteria of a person's technical ability, their resourcefulness in terms of ideas, and their commitment to the work. The two latter, of course, apply to the whole process over a period of time. If it is a large class, instead of having each person graded I may ask them in a secret ballot to nominate any members they feel have distinguished themselves, or failed to pull their weight. They are also asked to grade themselves. I then adjust *my* general category grading, applying minuses and plusses in a way that can stretch individual results outside that category. Thus it is conceivable for a C-graded product to have within it individuals with an A− and an F+. Students I have done this with seem to regard it as a fair way of working. It always astonishes me how much agreement there usually is within a group, especially in respect of which students should be given an A.

Continuous assessment

The Caloustie Gulbenkian Foundation (1982) recommends daily assessment, a feature of Canadian and American schools. My experience in those countries makes me feel reluctant to approve it as a practice, for in so many of their classrooms each child feels subjected to continual observation and grading by the teacher. The outcome is inevitably that the students come to see Drama as *about assessment*. The focus of attention is not directed towards 'meaning-making' as artists, but on whether or not the student will get an A for a particular piece of acting. So intent are students to catch the teacher's eye that their acting behaviour is automatically orientated towards the illustrative/performance mode, even when they are supposed to be behaving 'experientially', and if the teacher is looking the other way there seems to be little point in 'busting a gut'!

Yet the intention behind regular, illuminative, informal assessment seems sound. It is, after all, what we are doing most of the time we teach. Perhaps the mistake in North America is that such daily evaluation tends to be linked to grades. I think this is avoidable provided pupils understand from the beginning of a course that the idea of 'grading everything' is firmly excluded. We also need to find a form of continual assessment that gives credit to the participants' self-judgement. Only then can they begin to see themselves as artists in the classroom.

Bibliography

Berry, C. (1987) *The Actor and his Text* Harrap, London

Best, D. (1985) *Feeling and Reason in the Arts* George Allen & Unwin, London

Boal, A. (1979) *Theatre of the Oppressed* Pluto Press, London

Bolton, G. (1984) *Drama as Education: An Argument for Placing Drama at the Centre of the Curriculum* Longman, Harlow

—— (1986) 'The activity of dramatic playing' In: *Gavin Bolton: Selected Writings* (Eds D. Davis & C. Lawrence) Longman, London & New York

—— (1989) 'Drama' In: *Children and the Arts* (Ed. D. Hargreaves) Open University Press, Milton Keynes & Philadelphia

—— (1990) 'Four Aims in Teaching Drama' In: *London Drama* London Drama Association, London

—— (1990) 'Lernen durch und uber Drama im schulischen Unterricht' In: *Drama und Theater in der Schule und fur die Schule*, Universitat Oldenburg

Brecht, B. (1964) *Brecht on Theatre* (Ed. & Trs. J. Willet) Hill & Wang, New York

Bruner, J. (1971) *The Relevance of Education* Norton, New York

—— (1990) *Acts of Meaning* Harvard University Press, London

Caloustie Gulbenkian Foundation (1982) *The Arts in Schools* Caloustie Gulbenkian Foundation, London

Chapman, G. (1991) *Teaching Young Playwrights* Heinemann, New Hampshire

Davis, D. & Lawrence, C. (Eds) (1986) *Gavin Bolton: Selected Writings* Longman, London & New York

Department of Education and Science (1984) *English from 5 to 16: Curriculum Matters 1* HMSO, London

—— (1989) *Drama from 5 to 16: Curriculum Matters 17* HMSO, London

—— (1990) *The Teaching and Learning of Drama* (Aspects of Primary Education) HMSO, London

Johnson, E. & O'Neill, C. (1984) *Dorothy Heathcote: Collected Writings on Education and Drama* Hutchinson, London

Johnson, K. (1981) *Impro: Improvisation and Theatre* Methuen, London

Kempe, A. (1990) *The GCSE Drama Coursebook* Blackwell Education, Oxford

Laban, R. (1975) *A Life for Dance* MacDonald & Evans, London

Luria, A.R. & Yudovich, F.Y. (1959) *Speech and the Development of Mental Processes in the Child*, Staples Press

Landy, R. (1986) *Drama Therapy* Charles C. Thomas, Illinois

Maslow, A. (1954) *Motivation and Personality* Harper, New York

Morgan, N. & Saxton, J. (1991) *Teaching, Questioning and Learning* Routledge & Kegan Paul, London

National Curriculum Council (1990) *The Arts 5–16* Oliver & Boyd, York

O'Neill, C. & Lambert, A. (1982) *Drama Structures* Hutchinson, London

Perls, F. (1969) *Gestalt Therapy Verbatim* Real People Press, Moab
Polanyi, M. (1958) *Personal Knowledge: towards a Post-critical Philosophy*, Routledge & Kegan Paul, London
Rogers, C. (1961) *On Becoming a Person* Houghton-Mifflin, Boston
Sherbourne, V. (1990) *Developmental Movement in Children* Cambridge University Press, Cambridge
Slade, P. (1954) *Child Drama* University of London Press, London
Vygotsky, L. (1933) 'Play and its Role in the Mental Development of the Child' In: *Play* (Eds J.S. Bruner, et al.) Penguin Books (1976)
—— (1978) *Mind in Society, the Development of Higher Psychological Processes* Harvard University Press, London
Way, B. (1967) *Development through Drama* Longman, London
Serraillier, I. (1960) *The Silver Sword* Puffin, Harmondsworth, Middlesex

Index